THE BEST
QUIZ BOOK
OF THE WORLD

THE BEST
QUIZ BOOK
OF THE WORLD

Fun & Challenging Trivia Questions
on 111 Countries

TOM TRIFONOFF

To order additional copies of this book, contact:
Xlibris
1-800-455-039
www.Xlibris.com.au
Orders@Xlibris.com.au
800428

This book is dedicated to my family and friends who have supported, guided and encouraged me throughout this journey.

It is no surprise in this World Quiz book that they are truly people of the world, with ancestry from places such as England, Ireland, Bulgaria, Wales, Austria, Croatia, Germany, Switzerland, and Italy.

The world is a book,
and those
who do not travel
read only one page.

—Saint Augustine

INTRODUCTION

Welcome to **"The Best Quiz Book of the World"**-the only quiz book to have questions on specifically **111 countries** of the world. While other quiz books claim they are a world quiz book, which usually means they have questions about certain parts of the world, they do not cover individual countries like this book does.

Each country has 25 questions about it. These include the capital and largest cities, colours on the flag, prominent people, and type of government, its form of currency, sporting and cultural involvement and notable historic moments, to name just a few of the topics covered. Questions about population are simplified to give a range of 5 million when answering, and in most cases, the population is a recent estimate. Quizmasters can be quite flexible with close answers to the population questions. There are also specific questions that are only applicable to that country, but the majority of questions are reasonably easy, and also encourages people to have a guess, even if they may not know the answer.

The quiz is designed for people to learn more about their world by asking questions on 111 of the world's most well-known, influential or interesting countries. **"The Best Quiz Book of the World"** does what no other quiz book has done in the past-cover questions about so many countries from so many parts of the world. It is a very comprehensive look at our world.

At the end of each country's quiz, there are the answers to every question. The answers are correct at time of printing (July 2019) and while some statistics will change over time, it is designed to be accurate for a considerable amount of time. Sporting events, such as the Olympic Games, FIFA World Cup of Football, and Commonwealth Games are covered up their most recent tournament. Political events are also correct to the most recent time-but naturally are subject to change quite quickly-especially in some countries. All the countries are in alphabetical order for ease of reference.

There are **2775 questions** covering **111 countries** in **"The Best Quiz Book of the World"**. It does cover the large countries, the news making countries, some very small, but no less important countries, and some countries you may never have heard of before. And of course, there are **2775 answers** to those questions as well-all handily located at the end of each country's quiz-on the following page to stop prying eyes having a quick peek at the answers.

"The Best Quiz Book of the World" is a valuable and extremely informative reference book on many countries of the world. It would be a great source for quiz nights, family quizzes and very useful for senior primary school students and students in secondary school. It would be a valuable companion piece for English, Geography, Economics and History teachers.

The questions in **"The Best Quiz Book of the World"** designed to be easy and at times, challenging, but encouraging people to think through an answer, or at least have a guess on some of the more obscure questions. You may be surprised at how much you already know, and better still, how much you will learn from **"The Best Quiz Book of the World"**.

Enjoy the challenge and the answering of the world's truly first world quiz book-a book that asks questions on the widest range of topics about our world. I hope you enjoy **"The Best Quiz Book of the World"**.

Tom Trifonoff

FUN &
CHALLENGING
TRIVIA

QUESTIONS ON
111 COUNTRIES

AFGHANISTAN

1. What is the official name of Afghanistan?
2. What is the capital city of Afghanistan?
3. How many countries share a land border with Afghanistan?
4. What colours are on the flag of Afghanistan?
5. What is the main religion of Afghanistan?
6. What are the two official languages of Afghanistan?
7. Who is the Head of State in Afghanistan?
8. Which group ruled Afghanistan for over five years until forcibly removed in 2001?
9. What role did Afghanistan play during World War II?
10. What is the currency of Afghanistan?
11. What form of government did Afghanistan have for over 200 years, ending in 1973?
12. Who is the Head of Government in Afghanistan?
13. Between 30 and 35 million, what is the population of Afghanistan?
14. What is the largest city in Afghanistan?
15. Afghanistan is the world's leading illicit producer of which flowering plant?
16. What are the two most popular sports in Afghanistan?
17. Which side of the road do drivers in Afghanistan drive on?
18. Which country invaded Afghanistan in 1979?
19. What letters appear at the end of a web address from Afghanistan?
20. What form of government does Afghanistan have?
21. Which airline is the national carrier in Afghanistan?

22. In what year of the 2010s was the flag of Afghanistan adopted?
23. From which country did Afghanistan gain its independence from in 1919?
24. Which country is Afghanistan's major trading partner?
25. How many medals has Afghanistan won at the Summer Olympic Games?

AFGHANISTAN ANSWERS

1. Islamic Republic of Afghanistan
2. Kabul
3. Six-Pakistan, China, Uzbekistan, Iran, Turkmenistan, Tajikistan
4. Black, red, green
5. Islam
6. Dari, Pashto
7. President
8. Taliban
9. Neutral
10. Afghani
11. Monarchy
12. President
13. 32 million (2019 estimate)
14. Kabul
15. Opium
16. Cricket, football
17. Right hand side
18. Soviet Union
19. .af
20. Presidential Islamic Republic
21. Ariana Afghan Airlines
22. 2013
23. United Kingdom
24. Pakistan
25. Two-bronze (taekwondo)

ALBANIA

1. What is the official name of Albania?
2. What colours are on the flag of Albania?
3. What is the capital city of Albania?
4. How many countries share a land border with Albania?
5. From which country did Albania proclaim its independence in 1912?
6. What form of government does Albania have?
7. Which country invaded Albania in 1939?
8. Between one and five million, what is the population of Albania?
9. What is the currency of Albania?
10. What is the official language of Albania?
11. Who is the Head of State in Albania?
12. What is the national symbol of Albania?
13. Who is the Head of Government in Albania?
14. Which side of the road do drivers in Albania drive on?
15. Which country is Albania's major export partner?
16. What is the largest city in Albania?
17. What is Albania's main electricity source?
18. What is the national flower of Albania?
19. What is the most popular sport in Albania?
20. Which country is the major import partner of Albania?
21. How many medals has Albania won at the Summer Olympic Games?
22. What is the most popular spirit drink in Albania?

23. What letters appear at the end of a web address from Albania?
24. What is the best result Albania has had at the Eurovision Song Contest?
25. Who has been the only King of Albania?

ALBANIA ANSWERS

1. Republic of Albania
2. Red, black
3. Tirana
4. Four-Montenegro, Kosovo, Greece, Republic of North Macedonia
5. Ottoman Empire
6. Parliamentary constitutional republic
7. Italy
8. Two million (2.8 million)-(2017 estimate)
9. Lek
10. Albanian
11. President
12. Golden eagle
13. Prime Minister
14. Right hand side
15. Italy
16. Tirana
17. Hydropower
18. Red poppy
19. Football
20. Italy
21. None
22. Raki
23. .al
24. Fifth-2012
25. Zog I

ALGERIA

1. What is the formal name of Algeria?
2. What are the colours on the flag of Algeria?
3. What is the capital city of Algeria?
4. How many countries share a land border with Algeria?
5. Between 40 and 45 million, what is the population of Algeria?
6. From which country did Algeria gain its independence in 1962?
7. What are the two official languages of Algeria?
8. What form of government does Algeria have?
9. In terms of area, where does Algeria rank in size of countries in Africa?
10. What is the main export of Algeria?
11. Who is the Head of State in Algeria?
12. What is the most popular sport in Algeria?
13. What is the predominant religion in Algeria?
14. What is the main tourist attraction in Algeria?
15. Who is the Head of Government in Algeria?
16. What is the currency of Algeria?
17. Which country invaded Algeria in 1830?
18. Which side of the road do drivers in Algeria drive on?
19. What is the largest city in Algeria?
20. Which country is the major import partner of Algeria?
21. In which sport have Algerian sports people won the majority of their medals at the Summer Olympic Games?
22. Algerian born author Albert Camus won which prestigious literature award in 1957?

23. What letters appear at the end of a web address from Algeria?
24. Which country is Algeria's major export partner?
25. What day in July is Independence Day, a national holiday in Algeria?

ALGERIA ANSWERS

1. People's Democratic Republic of Algeria
2. Green, white, red
3. Algiers
4. Seven-Morocco, Niger, Tunisia, Libya, Mauritania, Mali, Western Sahara territory
5. 42 million (2018 estimate)
6. France
7. Berber, Arabic
8. Semi-presidential people's republic
9. Largest country in Africa
10. Petroleum products
11. President
12. Football
13. Islam
14. Sahara Desert
15. Prime Minister
16. Dinar
17. France
18. Right hand side
19. Algiers
20. China
21. Athletics
22. Nobel Prize for Literature
23. .dz
24. United States
25. July 5th

ANDORRA

1. What is the official name of Andorra?
2. In which continent is Andorra?
3. What is the capital of Andorra?
4. How many countries share a land border with Andorra?
5. What are the colours on the flag of Andorra?
6. What is the official language of Andorra?
7. Between 50000 and 100000, what is the population of Andorra?
8. From which country did Andorra gain its independence in 1814?
9. What form of government does Andorra have?
10. Which country provides the most tourists to Andorra?
11. What role did Andorra play in World War II?
12. Who is the Head of State in Andorra?
13. What is the main industry in Andorra?
14. What is the currency of Andorra?
15. Which country is the main export partner of Andorra?
16. What is the largest city in Andorra?
17. What is the dominant religious denomination in Andorra?
18. What is the most popular sport in Andorra?
19. Which side of the road do drivers in Andorra drive on?
20. How many airports are there in Andorra?
21. How many medals has Andorra won at the Summer Olympic Games?
22. Who is the Head of Government in Andorra?
23. Which country is the major import partner of Andorra?

24. What letters appear at the end of a web address from Andorra?

25. How many times has Andorra reached the final of the Eurovision Song Contest?

ANDORRA ANSWERS

1. Principality of Andorra
2. Europe
3. Andorra la Vella
4. Two-France, Spain
5. Red, yellow, blue
6. Catalan
7. 76000 (2019 estimate)
8. French Empire
9. Parliamentary semi-elective diarchy
10. Spain
11. Neutral
12. Co-Monarchs (Bishop of Urgell, President of France)
13. Tourism
14. Euro
15. Spain
16. Andorra la Vella
17. Roman Catholic
18. Football
19. Right hand side
20. None
21. None
22. Prime Minister
23. Spain
24. .ad
25. None

ARGENTINA

1. What is the official name of Argentina?
2. What are the colours on the flag of Argentina?
3. What is the capital city of Argentina?
4. How many countries share a land border with Argentina?
5. What form of government does Argentina have?
6. From which country did Argentina declare independence in 1816?
7. Between 40 and 45 million, what is the population of Argentina?
8. What role did Argentina play in the First and Second World Wars?
9. The invasion of the Falkland Islands in 1982 led to which war between Argentina and the United Kingdom?
10. Located in Argentina, which mountain is the highest in South America?
11. Who is the Head of State and Head of the Government in Argentina?
12. How many Argentinians have received the Nobel Prize in the sciences?
13. Which country provides the most tourists to Argentina?
14. What is the currency of Argentina?
15. What is the largest city in Argentina?
16. What is the national language of Argentina?
17. What is the most popular sport in Argentina?
18. How films from Argentina have won the Academy Award for Best Foreign Language Film?

19. How many times has Argentina won the FIFA World Cup of Football?
20. What symbol is in the middle of the flag of Argentina?
21. Which Argentine driver won the Formula One Grand Prix Championship five times?
22. Which side of the road do drivers in Argentina drive on?
23. What letters appear at the end of a web address from Argentina?
24. Who was President of Argentina in the 1940s and 1950s?
25. Who was the first Pope to come from Argentina?

ARGENTINA ANSWERS

1. Argentine Republic
2. Blue, white
3. Buenos Aires
4. Five-Brazil, Chile, Paraguay, Bolivia, Uruguay
5. Federal Presidential Constitutional Republic
6. Spain
7. 43 million (2016 estimate)
8. Neutral
9. Falklands War
10. Aconcagua
11. President
12. Three
13. Brazil
14. Peso
15. Buenos Aires
16. Spanish
17. Football
18. Two
19. Twice-1978, 1986
20. The sun
21. Juan Manuel Fangio
22. Right hand side
23. .ar
24. Juan Peron
25. Pope Francis

AUSTRALIA

1. What is the official name of Australia?
2. How many stars, in total, are on the Australian flag?
3. What is the capital city of Australia?
4. Which infamous Australian bushranger was hanged on November 11th 1880?
5. Between 20 and 25 million, what is the population of Australia?
6. Who is the Head of State of Australia?
7. What is the national language of Australia?
8. Which side of the road do Australian drivers drive on?
9. What is the currency of Australia?
10. In what year of the 20th century was the Federation of Australia?
11. Who was the first European to map the east coast of Australia?
12. Where in Australia is the world's largest coral reef?
13. What form of government does Australia have?
14. What letters appear at the end of a web address from Australia?
15. How many states and major mainland territories does Australia have in total?
16. What is the largest city in Australia?
17. What is the National Anthem of Australia?
18. What Australian film is regarded as the world's first feature length film?
19. What is the most popular spectator sport in Australia?

20. How many times has Australia hosted the Summer Olympic Games?
21. What form of coffee drink originated in Australia?
22. Which opera singer was the first Australian to achieve international recognition as a classical musician?
23. How many times has Australia won the cricket World Cup?
24. What was the first major military action by Australian soldiers?
25. Which explorer popularised the name Australia in the 19th century?

AUSTRALIA ANSWERS

1. Commonwealth of Australia
2. Six
3. Canberra
4. Ned Kelly
5. 25(.4) million (2019 estimate)
6. British Monarch
7. English
8. Left hand side
9. Australian dollar
10. 1901 (January 1st)
11. Captain James Cook
12. Great Barrier Reef-Queensland
13. Federal Parliamentary Constitutional Monarchy
14. .au
15. Eight-six states and two territories
16. Sydney
17. Advance Australia Fair
18. The Story of the Kelly Gang
19. Australian Rules Football
20. Twice-1956, 2000
21. Flat white
22. Dame Nellie Melba
23. Five times
24. Gallipoli Campaign in WWI
25. Matthew Flinders

AUSTRIA

1. What is the official national language of Austria?
2. What are the colours on the flag of Austria?
3. What is the capital city of Austria?
4. With which other country was there a dual sovereignty with Austria from 1867?
5. What is the currency of Austria?
6. Which country annexed Austria in 1938?
7. What is the official name of Austria?
8. Which mountain range is prominent in Austria?
9. More than half of Austria's electricity is generated by using what?
10. What is the dominant religious denomination of Austria?
11. Which famous composer was born in Salzburg Austria?
12. Which Austrian born actor became Governor of California?
13. Which Austrian Formula One driver was World Champion three times?
14. How many times have the Winter Olympics been held in Austria?
15. On which side of the road do Austrian drivers drive?
16. Which royal house ruled Austria until 1918?
17. Between five and ten million, what is the population of Austria?
18. What is the largest city in Austria?
19. What letters appear at the end of a web address from Austria?
20. Which male Austrian tennis player won the French Open in 1995?

21. From which country does Austria receive the most tourists?
22. What is the most visited landmark in Austria, with over 2 million visitors per year?
23. Which infamous 20th century dictator was born in Austria in 1889?
24. How many Academy Awards has Austrian born actor Christoph Waltz received?
25. How many times has Austria won the Eurovision Song Contest?

AUSTRIA ANSWERS

1. Austrian-German
2. Red and white
3. Vienna
4. Kingdom of Hungary
5. Euro
6. Germany
7. Republic of Austria
8. The Alps
9. Hydropower
10. Roman Catholic
11. Wolfgang Mozart
12. Arnold Schwarzenegger
13. Niki Lauder
14. Twice-1964, 1976
15. Right hand side
16. Habsburg
17. Eight million (8.8) (2018 estimate)
18. Vienna
19. .at
20. Thomas Muster
21. Germany
22. Schonbrunn Palace
23. Adolf Hitler
24. Two-Inglourious Basterds, Django Unchained
25. Twice-1966, 2014

BANGLADESH

1. What is the official name of Bangladesh?
2. What colours are on the flag of Bangladesh?
3. What is the capital city of Bangladesh?
4. How many countries share a land border with Bangladesh?
5. What was Bangladesh called before 1971?
6. What form of government does Bangladesh have?
7. Between 160 and 165 million, what is the population of Bangladesh?
8. What is the official religion of Bangladesh?
9. Who is the Head of State in Bangladesh?
10. What is the official language of Bangladesh?
11. Victory Day, a national holiday in Bangladesh, is celebrated on which day in December?
12. What is the currency of Bangladesh?
13. Who is the Head of Government in Bangladesh?
14. Which side of the road do drivers in Bangladesh drive on?
15. How many women have been Prime Minister of Bangladesh?
16. From which industry does Bangladesh derive most of its export earnings?
17. Which food is the staple of Bangladeshi cuisine?
18. What is the most popular sport in Bangladesh?
19. What is the largest city in Bangladesh?
20. How many medals has Bangladesh won at the Summer Olympic Games?
21. What is the national animal emblem of Bangladesh?
22. Which country is Bangladesh's largest trading partner?

23. What provides over half of Bangladesh's electrical needs?
24. How many Test matches has Bangladesh won since they started playing test cricket (as of July 2019)?
25. What letters appear at the end of a web address from Bangladesh?

BANGLADESH ANSWERS

1. People's Republic of Bangladesh
2. Red, green
3. Dhaka
4. Two-India, Myanmar
5. East Pakistan
6. Parliamentary republic
7. 162 million (2016 estimate)
8. Islam
9. President
10. Bengali
11. December 16th
12. Taka
13. Prime Minister
14. Left hand side
15. Two
16. Garment manufacturing
17. White rice
18. Cricket
19. Dhaka
20. None
21. Bengal tiger
22. India
23. Natural gas
24. Thirteen
25. .bd

BARBADOS

1. What is the capital city of Barbados?
2. What is the official name of Barbados?
3. What colours are on the flag of Barbados?
4. How many countries share a land border with Barbados?
5. What is the official language of Barbados?
6. From which country did Barbados gain its independence in 1966?
7. Between 100000 and 500000, what is the population of Barbados?
8. What form of government does Barbados have?
9. What is the dominant religious denomination in Barbados?
10. Who is the Head of State in Barbados?
11. Which country is the main export partner of Barbados?
12. What is the currency of Barbados?
13. What is the largest city in Barbados?
14. Which alcoholic drink is the most well-known in Barbados?
15. Who is the Head of Government in Barbados?
16. Which female singer, winner of nine Grammy Awards is Barbados's most famous musical export?
17. What is the most popular sport in Barbados?
18. Which side of the road do drivers in Barbados drive on?
19. Which day in November is the national holiday Independence Day?
20. Which country is the main import partner of Barbados?
21. What is the major industry in Barbados?
22. In which sport has Barbados won its only Summer Olympics medal-bronze, in 2000?

23. Which letters appear at the end of a web address from Barbados?
24. In which ocean is Barbados located?
25. Which cricket all-rounder, considered the greatest in the world, came from Barbados?

BARBADOS ANSWERS

1. Bridgetown
2. Barbados
3. Blue, gold, black
4. None
5. English
6. United Kingdom
7. 277000 (2010 census)
8. Parliamentary constitutional monarchy
9. Anglican
10. British monarch
11. Trinidad and Tobago
12. Barbadian dollar
13. Bridgetown
14. Rum
15. Prime Minister
16. Rhianna
17. Cricket
18. Left hand side
19. November 30th
20. Trinidad and Tobago
21. Tourism
22. Athletics
23. .bb
24. Atlantic Ocean
25. Sir Garfield Sobers

BELARUS

1. What is the official name of Belarus?
2. What colours are on the flag of Belarus?
3. What is the capital city of Belarus?
4. How many countries share a land border with Belarus?
5. Between five and ten million, what is the population of Belarus?
6. What are the two official languages of Belarus?
7. What form of government does Belarus have?
8. From which country did Belarus declare its independence in 1991?
9. What is the currency of Belarus?
10. Which country invaded Belarus in 1941?
11. Who is the Head of State in Belarus?
12. Which country is the major export partner of Belarus?
13. What is the largest city in Belarus?
14. What is the dominant religion in Belarus?
15. What is the most popular sport in Belarus?
16. What is the national dish of Belarus?
17. Which side of the road do drivers in Belarus drive on?
18. Who has been the most successful tennis player from Belarus, winning two grand slam titles?
19. What is the most popular tourist destination in Belarus?
20. How many gold medals has Belarus won at the Summer Olympic Games?
21. How many times has Belarus won the Eurovision Song Contest?
22. What is the largest export of Belarus?

23. How many other countries in Europe, apart from Belarus, also have capital punishment?
24. How many gold medals has Belarus won at the Winter Olympic Games?
25. What letters appear at the end of a web address from Belarus?

BELARUS ANSWERS

1. Republic of Belarus
2. Red, green, white
3. Minsk
4. Five-Russia, Lithuania, Ukraine, Poland, Latvia
5. Nine million (2018 estimate)
6. Belarusian, Russian
7. Presidential republic
8. USSR
9. Belarusian ruble
10. Germany
11. President
12. Russia
13. Minsk
14. Eastern Orthodox
15. Football
16. Draniki-potato pancake
17. Right hand side
18. Victoria Azarenka
19. Minsk
20. 12 gold medals
21. None-6th in 2007
22. Refined petroleum
23. None
24. Eight
25. .by

BELGIUM

1. What is the official name of Belgium?
2. What is the capital city of Belgium?
3. Between 10 and 15 million, what is the population of Belgium?
4. What are the colours on the flag of Belgium?
5. Which country did Belgium gain its independence from in 1830?
6. Who is the head of state in Belgium?
7. Which side of the road do Belgian drivers drive on?
8. What is the majority religion of Belgium?
9. What is the currency of Belgium?
10. What is the most popular sport in Belgium?
11. Which two Belgian female tennis players have been the most successful for their country?
12. What are the two national food dishes of Belgium?
13. Which beverage is Belgium most famous for?
14. How many times has Belgium won the Eurovision Song Contest?
15. What are the three official languages of Belgium?
16. What are the letters that appear at the end of a web address from Belgium?
17. How many countries does Belgium share a land border with?
18. What is the largest city in Belgium?
19. Which Belgian cyclist won the Tour de France five times in the 1960s and 1970s?

20. From which country does Belgium receive the most tourists?
21. Which country invaded Belgium in August 1914?
22. Which Belgian motor car driver won the Le Mans 24 Hour Race on six occasions?
23. How many times has Belgium hosted the Summer Olympic Games?
24. Which sweet food is Belgium famous for?
25. What type of government does Belgium have?

BELGIUM ANSWERS

1. Kingdom of Belgium
2. Brussels
3. Eleven million (2018 census)
4. Red, yellow and black
5. Netherlands
6. The monarch
7. Right hand side
8. Roman Catholicism
9. Euro
10. Football
11. Kim Clijsters, Justine Henin
12. Steak and fries, mussels with fries
13. Beer
14. Once-1986
15. French, German, Dutch
16. .be
17. Four-France, Germany, Luxembourg, Netherlands
18. Brussels
19. Eddie Merckx
20. Netherlands
21. Germany
22. Jacky Ickx
23. Once-Antwerp 1920
24. Chocolate
25. Federal Parliamentary Constitutional Monarchy

BOLIVIA

1. What is the capital of Bolivia?
2. What colours are on the flag of Bolivia?
3. What is the official name of Bolivia?
4. How many countries share a land border with Bolivia?
5. Between 10 and 15 million, what is the population of Bolivia?
6. What are the official languages of Bolivia?
7. What form of government does Bolivia have?
8. From which country did Bolivia gain its independence?
9. Bolivia has the world's largest concentration of which metal?
10. What is the currency of Bolivia?
11. Who is the Head of State in Bolivia?
12. Which mountain range runs through parts of Bolivia?
13. What is the main export commodity of Bolivia?
14. What is the largest city in Bolivia?
15. What is the most popular sport in Bolivia?
16. What is the dominant religious denomination in Bolivia?
17. Which country is Bolivia's major export partner?
18. Which side of the road do drivers in Brazil drive on?
19. Which country provides the most tourists to Bolivia?
20. Who is the Head of Government in Bolivia?
21. Which country is Bolivia's major import partner?
22. How many medals has Bolivia won at the Summer Olympic Games?

23. What letters appear at the end of a web address from Bolivia?
24. How many times has Bolivia qualified for the FIFA World Cup of football?
25. Which river runs through parts of Bolivia?

BOLIVIA ANSWERS

1. Sucre/La Paz
2. Red, yellow, green
3. Plurinational State of Bolivia
4. Five-Brazil, Peru, Chile, Paraguay, Argentina
5. 11 million (2019 estimate)
6. Spanish and 36 indigenous languages
7. Presidential constitutional republic
8. Spain
9. Lithium
10. Boliviano   .
11. President
12. Andes Mountains
13. Natural gas
14. Santa Cruz (de la Sierra)
15. Football
16. Roman Catholic
17. Brazil
18. Right hand side
19. Argentina
20. President
21. China
22. None
23. .bo
24. Three times-1930, 1950, 1994
25. Amazon River

BOSNIA & HERZEGOVINA

1. What is the capital city of Bosnia & Herzegovina?
2. What is the formal name of Bosnia & Herzegovina?
3. What colours are on the flag of Bosnia & Herzegovina?
4. How many countries share a land border with Bosnia & Herzegovina?
5. What are the three national languages of Bosnia & Herzegovina?
6. Geographically, what are locations of the areas Bosnia & Herzegovina?
7. What is the form of government in Bosnia & Herzegovina?
8. From which country did Bosnia & Herzegovina gain its independence in 1992?
9. Which body serves as the Head of State in Bosnia & Herzegovina?
10. Which two Empires had annexed Bosnia & Herzegovina in 1463, and then from 1878 to 1918?
11. What is the currency of Bosnia & Herzegovina?
12. What is the largest city in Bosnia & Herzegovina?
13. Between one and five million, what is the population of Bosnia & Herzegovina?
14. Which big sporting event was hosted by Bosnia & Herzegovina in 1984?
15. Which country provides the most tourists to Bosnia & Herzegovina?
16. What is the dominant religion in Bosnia & Herzegovina?
17. Who is the Head of Government in Bosnia & Herzegovina?

18. Which side of the road do drivers in Bosnia & Herzegovina drive on?

19. Which part of Bosnia & Herzegovina is most visited by tourists?

20. What is the best result Bosnia & Herzegovina has had at the Eurovision Song Contest?

21. Since becoming independent, how many medals has Bosnia & Herzegovina won at the Summer and Winter Olympic Games?

22. What letters appear at the end of a web address from Bosnia & Herzegovina?

23. How many Bosnia & Herzegovina born persons have been Nobel Prize laureates?

24. Which country is the major export partner of Bosnia & Herzegovina?

25. What is the most popular sport in Bosnia & Herzegovina?

BOSNIA & HERZEGOVINA ANSWERS

1. Sarajevo
2. Bosnia & Herzegovina
3. Blue, yellow, white
4. Three-Croatia, Serbia, Montenegro
5. Bosnian, Croatian, Serbian
6. Bosnia in the north; Herzegovina in the south
7. Parliamentary constitutional republic
8. Yugoslavia
9. Members of the Presidency- 3 member body
10. Ottoman Empire; Austro-Hungarian Monarchy
11. Convertible mark
12. Sarajevo
13. Three million (2013 census)
14. 14th Winter Olympics
15. Croatia
16. Islam
17. Chairman of the Council of Ministers
18. Right hand side
19. Sarajevo
20. Third-2006
21. None
22. .ba
23. Two-Literature, Chemistry
24. Germany
25. Football

BOTSWANA

1. What is the capital city of Botswana?
2. In which continent is Botswana?
3. What is the official name of Botswana?
4. What colours are on the flag of Botswana?
5. How many countries share a land border with Botswana?
6. What are the two official languages of Botswana?
7. What form of government does Botswana have?
8. From which country did Botswana gain its independence in 1966?
9. Between one and five million, what is the population of Botswana?
10. What is the currency of Botswana?
11. Who is the Head of State in Botswana?
12. Which country is the major export partner of Botswana?
13. What is the dominant religious denomination of Botswana?
14. What is the most popular sport in Botswana?
15. What is the main export commodity of Botswana?
16. Who is the Head of Government in Botswana?
17. Which side of the road do drivers in Botswana drive on?
18. What is the largest city in Botswana?
19. What day in September is the national holiday, Independence Day?
20. Which country is the major import partner of Botswana?
21. What letters appear at the end of a web address from Botswana?
22. Which country provides the most tourists to Botswana?

23. In which sport has Botswana won its only Summer Olympic Games medal-silver in 2012?
24. Which virus is in epidemic proportions in Botswana?
25. Botswana has the world's largest population of which large land animal?

BOTSWANA ANSWERS

1. Gaborone
2. Africa
3. Republic of Botswana
4. Blue, black, white
5. Four-South Africa, Namibia, Zambia, Zimbabwe
6. English, Setswana
7. Parliamentary republic
8. United Kingdom
9. Two million (2016 estimate)
10. Botswana pula
11. President
12. Belgium
13. Protestant
14. Football
15. Diamonds
16. President
17. Left hand side
18. Gaborone
19. September 30th
20. South Africa
21. .bw
22. South Africa
23. Athletics
24. HIV/AIDS
25. African elephant

BRAZIL

1. In terms of area, where does Brazil rank in terms of largest counties of the world?
2. What is the capital of Brazil?
3. What is the official name for Brazil?
4. What are the colours on the flag of Brazil?
5. What is the official language of Brazil?
6. How many countries share a land border with Brazil?
7. What form of government does Brazil have?
8. Brazil gained its independence from which country?
9. Which religion is the predominant faith of Brazil?
10. What is the currency of Brazil?
11. What is the largest city in Brazil?
12. Which side of the road do Brazilian drivers drive on?
13. What is the name of the world's largest rainforest, located in Brazil?
14. Who is both the Head of State and Head of Government in Brazil?
15. Which country provides the most tourists to Brazil?
16. What is the most popular sport in Brazil?
17. The Brazilian National holiday, Republic Day, is held in which day in November?
18. How many times has Brazil won the FIFA World Cup of Football?
19. How many times have Brazilian films won the Academy Award for Best foreign Language Film?
20. What is the national beverage of Brazil?
21. What letters appear at the end of a web page from Brazil?

22. Between 210 and 215 million, what is the population of Brazil?
23. Which driver is the most successful Brazilian in Formula One racing?
24. Which famous religious statue is located in Rio de Janeiro?
25. Which two lines of latitude run through Brazil?

BRAZIL ANSWERS

1. Fifth largest country in the world
2. Brasilia
3. Federative Republic of Brazil
4. Green, blue, yellow
5. Portuguese
6. 10-all other South American countries except Ecuador and Chile
7. Federal Presidential constitutional Republic
8. Portugal
9. Roman Catholic
10. Real
11. Sao Paulo
12. Right hand side
13. Amazon Rainforest
14. President
15. Argentina
16. Football
17. November 15th
18. Five times
19. None
20. Coffee
21. .br
22. 210 million (2019 estimate)
23. Ayrton Senna
24. Christ the Redeemer
25. Equator, Tropic of Capricorn

BULGARIA

1. What are the colours of the Bulgarian flag?
2. What is the currency of Bulgaria?
3. Who became the first male Bulgarian tennis player to be ranked in the Top 10 ATP rankings?
4. What has been the best performance by the Bulgarian football team at the FIFA World Cup?
5. What is the capital of Bulgaria?
6. On which side did Bulgaria fight in the First World War?
7. What is type of alphabet used in Bulgaria?
8. What is the formal name of Bulgaria?
9. Who was the last full ruling Tsar of Bulgaria?
10. Between five and ten million, what is the population of Bulgaria?
11. Bulgaria is the world's largest producer of which oils used in fragrances?
12. In what year was the monarchy abolished in Bulgaria?
13. What is the largest city in Bulgaria?
14. What is the official language of Bulgaria?
15. Who is credited with developing the Bulgarian alphabet?
16. On what date in March does Bulgaria celebrate National Liberation Day?
17. The Bulgarian Black Sea Coast, known for its high tourism, has what nickname?
18. In what year was there the end of Communist monopoly rule in Bulgaria?
19. How many letters are there in the Bulgarian alphabet?
20. What side of the road do Bulgarians drive on?

21. Which empire ruled over Bulgaria for nearly 500 years?
22. From which European country does Bulgaria attract the most tourists each year (as of 2017)?
23. What is the Bulgarian sculptor Christo mostly famous for?
24. How many countries share a land border with Bulgaria?
25. What letters are used at the end of a Bulgarian internet address?

BULGARIA ANSWERS

1. White, green, red
2. Bulgarian lev
3. Grigor Dimitrov
4. Semi-finals 1994
5. Sofia
6. Central Powers
7. Cyrillic alphabet
8. Republic of Bulgaria
9. Boris III
10. 7 million (2018 estimate)
11. Lavender and rose oil
12. 1946
13. Sofia
14. Bulgarian
15. Saints Cyril and Methodius
16. March 3rd
17. Bulgarian Riviera
18. 1989
19. 30
20. Right hand side
21. Ottoman Empire
22. Romania
23. Wrapping of monuments, objects-environmental art
24. Five-Romania, Serbia, Turkey, Greece, Republic of Macedonia
25. .bg

CAMBODIA

1. What is the official religion of Cambodia?
2. What is the capital city of Cambodia?
3. How many countries share a land border with Cambodia?
4. What colours are on the flag of Cambodia?
5. What is the official name of Cambodia?
6. From which country did Cambodia gain its independence in 1953?
7. What form of government does Cambodia have?
8. What is the official language of Cambodia?
9. Which political group ruled Cambodia between 1975 and 1979 and carried out mass genocide in that time?
10. Which country is the major export partner of Cambodia?
11. Which country provides the most tourists to Cambodia?
12. Which non-alcoholic drink is consumed most by people in Cambodia?
13. Who is the Head of State in Cambodia?
14. What is the most popular sport in Cambodia?
15. What is the currency in Cambodia?
16. What is the largest city in Cambodia?
17. Between 15 and 20 million, what is the population of Cambodia?
18. What industry is the largest in Cambodia?
19. Who is the Head of Government in Cambodia?
20. Which country is the major import partner of Cambodia?
21. Who was the leader of Cambodia from 1975 to 1975 which saw mass genocide committed?
22. Which side of the road do drivers in Cambodia drive on?

23. How many medals has Cambodia won at the Summer Olympic Games?
24. Which 1984 film depicted Cambodia during the 1975-79 period of genocide?
25. What letters appear at the end of a website from Cambodia?

CAMBODIA ANSWERS

1. Buddhism
2. Phnom Penh
3. Three-Thailand, Laos, Vietnam
4. Red, blue
5. Kingdom of Cambodia
6. France
7. Dominant party parliamentary elective constitutional monarchy
8. Khmer
9. Khmer Rouge
10. United States of America
11. China
12. Tea
13. Monarch (King)
14. Football
15. Riel
16. Phnom Penh
17. 16 million (2019 estimate)
18. Textile industry
19. Prime Minister
20. China
21. Pol Pot
22. Right hand side
23. None
24. The Killing Fields
25. .kh

CAMEROON

1. What is the capital city of Cameroon?
2. What colours are on the flag of Cameroon?
3. How many countries share a land border with Cameroon?
4. What is the official name of Cameroon?
5. What are the official languages of Cameroon?
6. What type of government does Cameroon have?
7. From which country did Cameroon declare its independence in 1960?
8. Between 20 and 25 million, what is the population of Cameroon?
9. What is the dominant religious denomination in Cameroon?
10. What is the most popular sport in Cameroon?
11. Who is the Head of State in Cameroon?
12. How many times has Cameroon won the African Cup of Nations football title?
13. Which country is Cameroon's major import partner?
14. Which side of the road do drivers in Cameroon drive on?
15. Who is the Head of Government in Cameroon?
16. What is the currency of Cameroon?
17. What is the main export commodity of Cameroon?
18. Which country provides the most tourists to Cameroon?
19. What is the largest city in Cameroon?
20. Who is probably Cameroon's best known football player?
21. What letters appear at the end of a web address from Cameroon?
22. What medal did the Cameroon football team win at the 2000 Olympic Games?

23. Cameroon was a colony of which country before World War One?
24. Which country is the major export partner of Cameroon?
25. In which sport did Francoise Mbango Etone win two gold medals at the 2004 and 2008 Summer Olympic Games?

CAMEROON ANSWERS

1. Yaounde
2. Red, green, yellow
3. Six-Chad, Nigeria, Republic of the Congo, Equatorial Guinea, Gabon, Central African Republic
4. Republic of Cameroon
5. French, English
6. Presidential republic under a totalitarian dictatorship
7. France
8. 23 million (2016 estimate)
9. Roman Catholic
10. Football
11. President
12. Five times
13. China
14. Right hand side
15. Prime Minister-but mainly President
16. Central African CFA franc
17. Crude oil and petroleum products
18. France
19. Douala
20. Roger Milla
21. .cm
22. Gold medal
23. Germany
24. The Netherlands
25. Women's triple jump

CANADA

1. What are the colours on the flag of Canada?
2. What is the capital city of Canada?
3. What are the two official languages of Canada?
4. Between 35 and 40 million, what is the population of Canada?
5. What form of Government does Canada have?
6. Who became Prime Minister of Canada in 2015?
7. What are the two official sports of Canada?
8. Which side of the road do Canadian drivers drive on?
9. What is the currency of Canada?
10. Who is Canada's highest selling music artist?
11. How many times has Canada hosted the Summer Olympic Games?
12. What symbol is on the Canadian flag?
13. What is the largest city in Canada?
14. Chris Hadfield became the first Canadian to do what in 2001?
15. Which Canadian territory is comprised mainly by the Inuit people?
16. Who is the Head of State in Canada?
17. What letters appear at the end of a web address from Canada?
18. On which day in July is Canada Day, Canada's National Day?
19. Where does Canada rank in terms of size of the largest countries in the world?
20. Which country provides the most tourists to Canada?
21. How many times has Canada hosted the Winter Olympics?

22. How many Nobel Prize laureates have come from Canada?
23. How many Provinces and Territories are there in total in Canada?
24. Which Province in Canada is predominantly French speaking?
25. What is the largest religious denomination in Canada?

CANADA ANSWERS

1. Red and white
2. Ottawa
3. English, French
4. 37 million (2019 estimate)
5. Federal Parliamentary Constitutional Monarchy
6. Justin Trudeau
7. Ice hockey, lacrosse
8. Right hand side
9. Canadian dollar
10. Celine Dion
11. Once-1976
12. Maple leaf
13. Toronto
14. Walk in space
15. Nunavut
16. British Monarch
17. .ca
18. July 1st
19. Second largest in total area
20. United States
21. Twice-1988, 2010
22. Thirteen (as of 2015)
23. Ten Provinces, three Territories
24. Quebec
25. Roman Catholic

CHILE

1. What is the capital city of Chile?
2. What is the official name of Chile?
3. How many countries share a land border with Chile?
4. What colours are on the flag of Chile?
5. What is the national language of Chile?
6. Which country did Chile gain its independence from?
7. What form of government does Chile have?
8. What is the currency of Chile?
9. Who is the Head of State in Chile?
10. Who ruled Chile as a dictator from 1973 to 1990?
11. Which country is the major export partner of Chile?
12. What is the largest city in Chile?
13. What are the two national animals of Chile?
14. Which desert is found in Chile?
15. Between 15 and 20 million, what is the population of Chile?
16. What is the dominant religious denomination in Chile?
17. What is the biggest export of Chile?
18. Which country provides the most tourists to Chile?
19. What is the most popular sport in Chile?
20. How many times has a film from Chile won the Academy Award for Best Foreign Language Film?
21. What has been Chile's most successful sport at the Summer Olympic Games, with two gold medals?
22. Which side of the road do drivers in Chile drive on?
23. What letters appear at the end of a web address from Chile?
24. Who is the Head of Government in Chile?
25. How many Nobel Prize laureates has Chile had?

CHILE ANSWERS

1. Santiago
2. Republic of Chile
3. Three-Peru, Bolivia, Argentina
4. Red, white, blue
5. Spanish
6. Spain
7. Presidential constitutional republic
8. Peso
9. President
10. Augusto Pinochet
11. China
12. Santiago
13. Condor, huemul (white tail deer)
14. Atacama Desert
15. 17 million (2017 census)
16. Roman Catholic
17. Copper
18. Argentina
19. Football
20. Once-2017
21. Tennis
22. Right hand side
23. .cl
24. President
25. Two

CHINA

1. What is the capital city of China?
2. What is the official name for China?
3. What colours are on the flag of China?
4. What is the official language of China?
5. What is China's national symbol?
6. In what year of the 1980s did China hit the one billion mark in its population?
7. How many stars are on the flag of China?
8. What form of government is established in China?
9. What is the largest city in China?
10. What was the name of the last imperial dynasty to rule China?
11. What is the currency of China?
12. Which country invaded China in 1937?
13. Which side of the road do Chinese drivers drive on?
14. What letters are at the end of a web address from China?
15. What is the most popular spectator sport in China?
16. What are the Four Great Inventions invented by the Chinese during ancient times and noted for their significance on civilisation?
17. Who became leader of China in 1949?
18. Who is the highest ranking official in the Chinese government?
19. In what year did the Chinese city of Beijing host the Summer Olympic Games?
20. How many time zones does China have?

21. What is the popular name of the island that is officially known as the Republic of China?
22. What is the main environmental health issue affecting China?
23. How many countries share a land border with China?
24. Not including Chinese regions and territories and Taiwan, which country provides the most tourists to China?
25. What is the most visited site in China by tourists?

CHINA ANSWERS

1. Beijing
2. People's Republic of China
3. Red and yellow
4. Standard Chinese (Mandarin)
5. Dragon
6. 1980
7. Five
8. Marxist-Leninist one party socialist republic
9. Shanghai
10. Qing Dynasty
11. Renminbi (Yuan)
12. Japan
13. Right hand side
14. .cn
15. Basketball
16. Compass, gunpowder, paper making, printing
17. Mao Zedong
18. General Secretary
19. 2008
20. One
21. Taiwan
22. Air pollution
23. Fourteen
24. South Korea
25. Great Wall of China

COLOMBIA

1. What is the capital of Colombia?
2. What colours are on the flag of Colombia?
3. What is the official name of Colombia?
4. What form of government does Colombia have?
5. How many countries share a land border with Colombia?
6. Between 45 and 50 million, what is the population of Colombia?
7. What is the official language of Colombia?
8. From which country did Colombia declare its independence?
9. Which country seceded from Colombia in 1903?
10. What is the currency of Colombia?
11. Colombia was the only South American country to be involved in which conflict of the 1950s?
12. Who is the Head of State in Colombia?
13. What is the largest city in Colombia?
14. From what is nearly 70% of Colombia's electricity generated?
15. What is the dominant religious denomination in Colombia?
16. Who is Colombia's most successful musical export?
17. What is the most popular sport in Colombia?
18. Which side of the road do drivers in Colombia drive on?
19. Which country provides the most tourists to Colombia?
20. How many Colombians have been awarded a Nobel Prize?
21. What is the national sport of Colombia?
22. In which two sports has Colombia won the most gold medals at the Summer Olympic Games (as of 2016)?

23. Who is the Head of Government in Colombia?
24. What letters appear at the end of a web address from Colombia?
25. What is the biggest export of Colombia?

COLOMBIA ANSWERS

1. Bogota
2. Red, blue, yellow
3. Republic of Colombia
4. Presidential constitutional republic
5. Five-Panama, Ecuador, Brazil, Peru, Venezuela
6. 48 million (2019 estimate)
7. Spanish
8. Spain
9. Panama
10. Peso
11. Korean War
12. President
13. Bogota
14. Hydroelectric power
15. Roman Catholic
16. Shakira
17. Football
18. Right hand side
19. Venezuela
20. Two-Literature, Peace
21. Tejo
22. Weightlifting, cycling
23. President
24. .co
25. Crude petroleum

CROATIA

1. What is the official name for Croatia?
2. What is the capital city of Croatia?
3. How many countries share a land border with Croatia?
4. What colours are on the flag of Croatia?
5. Between one and five million, what is the population of Croatia?
6. What is the official language of Croatia?
7. From which country did Croatia declare its independence in 1991?
8. What form of government does Croatia have?
9. What is the currency of Croatia?
10. Who is the Head of State in Croatia?
11. Which country provides the most tourists to Croatia?
12. What is the dominant religious denomination of Croatia?
13. What is the largest city in Croatia?
14. Which side of the road do drivers in Croatia drive on?
15. Which country is the major export partner of Croatia?
16. What is the most popular sport in Croatia?
17. How many times has Croatia won the Davis Cup in tennis?
18. What letters appear at the end of a web address from Croatia?
19. Who is the Patron Saint of Croatia?
20. Who is the Head of Government in Croatia?
21. What has been the best placed finish for Croatia at the Eurovision Song Contest?
22. Where did Croatia finish in the 2018 FIFA World Cup of football?

23. What has been the most successful sport for Croatia at the Winter Olympics?

24. Which Croatian city was used for filming on Game of thrones and Star Wars: The Last Jedi?

25. Which Croatian football player won the Ballon d'Or award in 2018?

CROATIA ANSWERS

1. Republic of Croatia
2. Zagreb
3. Five-Serbia, Slovenia, Bosnia and Herzegovina, Republic of Macedonia, Hungary
4. Red, white, blue
5. 4 million (2019 estimate)
6. Croatian
7. Yugoslavia
8. Parliamentary constitutional republic
9. Kuna
10. President
11. Germany
12. Roman Catholic
13. Zagreb
14. Right hand side
15. Italy
16. Football
17. Twice-2005, 2018
18. .hr
19. St Joseph
20. Prime Minister
21. Fourth-1996, 1999
22. Runners-up
23. Alpine ski-ing
24. Dubrovnik
25. Luka Modric

CUBA

1. What is the official name of Cuba?
2. What is the capital of Cuba?
3. What is the official language of Cuba?
4. Who led the Cuban Revolution and became leader of the country in 1959?
5. Which country gained control of Cuba after the Spanish-American War of 1898?
6. Between 10 and 15 million, what is the population of Cuba?
7. What was the name of the CIA plan to overthrow the government of Cuba in 1961?
8. What is the currency for Cuba?
9. What letters appear at the end of a web address from Cuba?
10. What colours are on the flag of Cuba?
11. In terms of area what rank is Cuba in relation to the sizes of the Caribbean Islands?
12. What is the minimum voting age in Cuba?
13. What is the largest religion in Cuba?
14. Which side of the road do Cuban drivers drive on?
15. What is the most popular sport played in Cuba?
16. How many gold medals did Cuban boxer Teofilo Stevenson win at his three Olympic Games?
17. What is the largest city in Cuba?
18. During the three decades after 1959, what percentage of Cubans emigrated to the United States?
19. How many islands in total make up the island of Cuba?
20. From which country does Cuba receive the most tourists?

21. Who was the Cuban dictator that was deposed in 1959?
22. What is the name of the political party that governs Cuba?
23. How many Popes have visited Cuba?
24. Which hurricane hit Cuba in September 2017?
25. How many stars are on the flag of Cuba?

CUBA ANSWERS

1. Republic of Cuba
2. Havana
3. Spanish
4. Fidel Castro
5. United States of America
6. 11 million (2018 census)
7. Bay of Pigs Invasion
8. Peso
9. .cu
10. Red, white, blue
11. Largest island
12. Sixteen
13. Catholicism
14. Right hand side
15. Baseball
16. Three
17. Havana
18. 10%
19. Five
20. Canada
21. Fulgencio Batista
22. Communist Party of Cuba
23. Three-Pope John Paul II, Pope Benedict XVI, Pope Francis
24. Hurricane Irma
25. One

CZECH REPUBLIC

1. What is the official name of the Czech Republic?
2. What is the capital city of the Czech Republic?
3. What are the colours on the flag of the Czech Republic?
4. How many countries share a land border with the Czech Republic?
5. Between five and ten million, what is the population of the Czech Republic?
6. What is the currency of the Czech Republic?
7. What form of government does the Czech Republic have?
8. In what year of the 1990s did Czech Republic and Slovakia become separate countries?
9. Who is the patron saint of Czech Republic?
10. Who is the Head of State in the Czech Republic?
11. What is the largest city in Czech Republic?
12. Which large car manufacturer is based in Czech Republic?
13. How many Czechs have won a Nobel Prize?
14. Which side of the road do Czech Republic drivers drive on?
15. Which Czech Republic city is the most visited by tourists?
16. What is the official language of the Czech Republic?
17. What are the two leading sports in Czech Republic?
18. Which form of beer originated in the Czech Republic city of Plzen?
19. How many Czech films have won the Academy Award for Best Foreign Language Film?
20. What larger country were Czech Republic and Slovakia part of before it was dissolved?

21. Which Czech football player has been a goalkeeper for Premier League teams Chelsea and Arsenal?

22. What letters appear at the end of a web address from Czech Republic?

23. Which country provides the most tourists to Czech Republic?

24. Who is the Head of Government in Czech Republic?

25. At which sport has Czech Republic won the most Summer Olympic Gold Medals?

CZECH REPUBLIC ANSWERS

1. Czech Republic
2. Prague
3. Red, white, blue
4. Four-Germany, Austria, Slovakia, Poland
5. 10 (.6)million (2019 estimate)
6. Czech koruna
7. Parliamentary constitutional republic
8. 1993
9. St Wenceslas
10. President
11. Prague
12. Skoda
13. Five
14. Right hand side
15. Prague
16. Czech
17. Ice hockey, football
18. Pilsner
19. Three
20. Czechoslovakia
21. Petr Cech
22. .cz
23. Germany
24. Prime Minister
25. Athletics

DENMARK

1. What is the official name of Denmark?
2. What are the colours on the flag of Denmark?
3. What is the capital city of Denmark?
4. Which country shares a natural land border with Denmark?
5. What form of government does Denmark have?
6. What is the National Church of Denmark?
7. Which country invaded Denmark during the Second World War?
8. What is the currency of Denmark?
9. Which side of the road do Danish drivers drive on?
10. Between one and five million, what is the population of Denmark?
11. What is the official language of Denmark?
12. What is the national sport of Denmark?
13. What is the largest city in Denmark?
14. The Oresund Bridge links Denmark with which other country?
15. What letters appear at the end of a web address from Denmark?
16. Which two territories, autonomous constituent countries, are parts of Denmark?
17. What part did Denmark play in World War I?
18. Who is the Head of State of Denmark?
19. How many times has Denmark won the Eurovision Song Contest?
20. Which country provides the most tourists to Denmark?

21. How many times has Denmark won the UEFA European Football Championship?
22. Which Danish writer is most famous for his fairy tales?
23. How many times have Danish films won the Academy Award for Best Foreign Language Film?
24. What is the largest island of Denmark?
25. What is the most recognisable beer to come from Denmark?

DENMARK ANSWERS

1. Kingdom of Denmark
2. Red and white
3. Copenhagen
4. Germany
5. Parliamentary Constitutional Monarchy
6. Church of Denmark (Evangelical Lutheran Church in Denmark)
7. Germany
8. Danish krone
9. Right hand side
10. Five million (2018 estimate)
11. Danish
12. Football
13. Copenhagen
14. Sweden
15. .dk
16. Greenland, Faroe Islands
17. Neutral
18. The Monarch
19. Three times
20. Germany
21. Once-1992
22. Hans Christian Andersen
23. Three times
24. Zealand
25. Carlsberg

ECUADOR

1. What is the capital city of Ecuador?
2. How many countries share a border with Ecuador?
3. What colours are on the flag of Ecuador?
4. In which continent is Ecuador?
5. What is the official name for Ecuador?
6. What is the official language of Ecuador?
7. What form of government does Ecuador have?
8. From which country did Ecuador gain its independence in 1822?
9. Between 15 and 20 million, what is the population of Ecuador?
10. What is Ecuador's major export?
11. Who is the Head of State in Ecuador?
12. Which mountain range runs through Ecuador?
13. What is the most popular tourist destination of Ecuador?
14. Which country is the major export partner of Ecuador?
15. What is the dominant religious denomination in Ecuador?
16. What is the currency of Ecuador?
17. What is the largest city in Ecuador?
18. Who is the Head of Government in Ecuador?
19. What is the most popular sport in Ecuador?
20. Which side of the road do drivers in Ecuador drive on?
21. Which ocean has a border with Ecuador?
22. How many medals has Ecuador won at the Summer Olympic Games?
23. Which country is the major import partner of Ecuador?

24. What letters appear at the end of a web address from Ecuador?
25. How many times has Ecuador qualified for the FIFA World Cup of Football?

ECUADOR ANSWERS

1. Quito
2. Two-Colombia, Peru
3. Red, yellow, blue
4. South America
5. Republic of Ecuador
6. Spanish
7. Presidential constitutional republic
8. Spain
9. 16 million (2016 estimate)
10. Oil (Petroleum products)
11. President
12. The Andes
13. Galapagos Islands
14. United States of America
15. Roman Catholic
16. US dollar
17. Quito
18. President
19. Football
20. Right hand side
21. Pacific Ocean
22. Two-gold, silver by walker Jefferson Perez
23. United States of America
24. .ec
25. Three times-2002, 2006, 2014

EGYPT

1. What is the official name for Egypt?
2. What is the capital city of Egypt?
3. What are the colours on the flag of Egypt?
4. How many countries share a land border with Egypt?
5. What is the official language of Egypt?
6. What is the official religion of Egypt?
7. Where in Egypt are many of the tombs of Egyptian pharaohs located?
8. What form of government does Egypt have?
9. Which country is the major export partner of Egypt?
10. From which country did Egypt gain its independence in 1922?
11. What is the currency of Egypt?
12. Who is considered the greatest of all the Egyptian pharaohs, with a reign of over 66 years?
13. What is the largest city in Egypt?
14. What is the major tourist destination of Egypt?
15. Which famous artificial waterway in Egypt was opened in 1869?
16. What is the name of the Ancient Egyptian writing system made up of characters?
17. Which side of the road do Egyptian drivers drive on?
18. Between 90 and 95 million, what is the population of Egypt?
19. What is the most popular national sport in Egypt?
20. Egypt is considered the home of which form of dance?

21. What letters appear at the end of a web address from Egypt?
22. Which pharaoh's tomb was discovered undisturbed in 1922?
23. How many times has the Egyptian national football team won the African Cup of Nations title?
24. Who is the Head of State in Egypt?
25. Which river is the primary water source of Egypt?

EGYPT ANSWERS

1. Arab Republic of Egypt
2. Cairo
3. Red, white, black
4. Three-Israel, Sudan, Libya
5. Arabic
6. Islam
7. Valley of the Kings
8. Semi Presidential Republic
9. United Arab Emirates
10. United Kingdom
11. Egyptian pound
12. Ramses II
13. Cairo
14. Great Pyramid of Giza
15. Suez Canal
16. Hieroglyphics
17. Right hand side
18. 94 million (2017 census)
19. Football
20. Belly dance
21. .eg
22. Tutankhamen
23. Seven times
24. President
25. Nile River

EL SALVADOR

1. What is the capital city of El Salvador?
2. What colours are on the flag of El Salvador?
3. What is the official name of El Salvador?
4. How many countries share a land border with El Salvador?
5. Between five and ten million, what is the population of El Salvador?
6. What form of government does El Salvador have?
7. What is the official language of El Salvador?
8. What is the currency of El Salvador?
9. Which country did El Salvador declare its independence from in 1821?
10. What is the geographical region where El Salvador is located called?
11. What is the largest city in El Salvador?
12. Who is the Head of State in El Salvador?
13. Which country is the major export partner of El Salvador?
14. What is the dominant religious denomination of El Salvador?
15. Where does El Salvador rate in terms of murder rate in the world?
16. What is the national dish of El Salvador?
17. What is the most popular sport in El Salvador?
18. Which side of the road do drivers in El Salvador drive on?
19. Which country ruled El Salvador for nearly 300 years?
20. Which country is El Salvador's major import partner?
21. What day in September is Independence Day, a national holiday in El Salvador?

22. How many times has El Salvador qualified for the FIFA World Cup?
23. What letters appear at the end of a web address from El Salvador?
24. Which two natural disasters hit El Salvador the most?
25. Who is the Head of Government in El Salvador?

EL SALVADOR ANSWERS

1. San Salvador
2. Blue, white
3. Republic of El Salvador
4. Two-Honduras, Guatemala
5. 6 million (2016 estimate)
6. Presidential constitutional republic
7. Spanish
8. US dollar
9. Spain
10. Central America
11. San Salvador
12. President
13. United States
14. Roman Catholic
15. Highest murder rate in the world
16. Pupusa-corn tortilla filled with savoury filling
17. Football
18. Right hand side
19. Spain
20. United States
21. September 15th
22. Twice-1970, 1982
23. .sv
24. Earthquakes, volcanic eruptions
25. President

ESTONIA

1. What is the official name of Estonia?
2. What colours are on the flag of Estonia?
3. What is the capital city of Estonia?
4. How many countries share a land border with Estonia?
5. Between one and five million, what is the population of Estonia?
6. What is the currency of Estonia?
7. What form of government does Estonia have?
8. What is the official language of Estonia?
9. Which two countries occupied Estonia from 1940 to 1991?
10. Who is the Head of State in Estonia?
11. Which country is the major export partner of Estonia?
12. What is the major religious denomination in Estonia?
13. How many times has Estonia won the Eurovision Song Contest?
14. Estonia's national day, Independence Day, is held on which day in February?
15. Who is the Head of Government in Estonia?
16. What is the largest city in Estonia?
17. What is the most popular sport in Estonia?
18. Which country is the major import partner of Estonia?
19. Which side of the road do drivers in Estonia drive on?
20. In which sport has Estonia been most successful at the Summer Olympic Games?
21. What letters appear at the end of a web address from Estonia?
22. What is the most popular tourist destination in Estonia?

23. At which sport has Estonia been most successful at the Winter Olympic Games?
24. Which country provides the most tourists to Estonia?
25. Kersti Kaljulaid became the first what of Estonia in 2016?

ESTONIA ANSWERS

1. Republic of Estonia
2. Blue, black, white
3. Tallinn
4. Two-Russia, Latvia
5. One(.3)million (2019 estimate)
6. Euro
7. Parliamentary republic
8. Estonian
9. Germany, Soviet Union
10. President
11. Finland
12. Lutheran
13. Once-2001
14. February 24th
15. Prime Minister
16. Tallinn
17. Football
18. Finland
19. Right hand side
20. Wrestling
21. .ee
22. Tallinn
23. Cross country skiing
24. Finland
25. First female President

ETHIOPIA

1. What is the official name of Ethiopia?
2. What is the capital city of Ethiopia?
3. How many countries share a border with Ethiopia?
4. What colours are on the flag of Ethiopia?
5. Between 100 and 105 million, what is the population of Ethiopia?
6. What is the official language of Ethiopia?
7. Which country invaded Ethiopia in 1936?
8. What was the former name of Ethiopia?
9. Prior to 1974, Ethiopia was ruled by what form of government?
10. Which country is the major export partner of Ethiopia?
11. What is the currency of Ethiopia?
12. With over 88% of capacity what is the leading electricity provider in Ethiopia?
13. What is the most widely spoken foreign language in Ethiopia?
14. What are the two main sports in Ethiopia?
15. Which side of the road do drivers from Ethiopia drive on?
16. What letters appear at the end of a web address sent from Ethiopia?
17. How many World Heritage sites are there in Ethiopia?
18. What is the largest city in Ethiopia?
19. Who ruled Ethiopia from 1930 to 1974?
20. Who was the first sitting US President to visit Ethiopia?
21. At which Olympic event have Ethiopian athletes dominated over the years?

22. What time does the Ethiopian day start?
23. Which airline is Ethiopia's flag carrier?
24. What is Ethiopia's main export?
25. Who is the Head of Government in Ethiopia?

ETHIOPIA ANSWERS

1. Federal Democratic Republic of Ethiopia
2. Addis Ababa
3. Six-Eritrea, Sudan, South Sudan, Kenya, Somalia, Djibouti
4. Green, yellow, red
5. 102 million (2016 estimate)
6. Amharic
7. Italy
8. Abyssinia
9. Monarchy
10. Sudan
11. Birr
12. Hydroelectric power
13. English
14. Track and field, football
15. Right hand side
16. .et
17. Nine
18. Addis Ababa
19. Haile Selassie
20. Barack Obama
21. Long distance running
22. 6 am
23. Ethiopian Airlines
24. Coffee
25. Prime Minister

FIJI

1. What is the official name of Fiji?
2. What is the capital city of Fiji?
3. In which ocean is Fiji?
4. What form of government does Fiji have?
5. What colours are on the flag of Fiji?
6. Between 500000 and one million, what is the population of Fiji?
7. What are the three official languages of Fiji?
8. From which country did Fiji gain its independence in 1970?
9. Who is the Head of Government in Fiji?
10. What is the currency of Fiji?
11. Which Dutch explorer was the first known European to visit Fiji?
12. Approximately what fraction of Fiji's islands is inhabited?
13. Which country provides the most tourists to Fiji?
14. What is the leading economic activity of Fiji?
15. Who is the Head of Government in Fiji?
16. What is the main religious denomination in Fiji?
17. What is Fiji's national sport?
18. What day in October is the holiday Fiji Day?
19. Which side of the road do drivers in Fiji drive on?
20. What is the largest city in Fiji?
21. In what year of the 2000s was the coup by the military in Fiji?
22. What is the most popular sport in Fiji?
23. What letters appear at the end of a web address from Fiji?

24. Which cyclone that hit Fiji in December 2009 killed four people?

25. In which sport did Fiji win its first gold medal at the Summer Olympic Games?

FIJI ANSWERS

1. Republic of Fiji
2. Suva
3. Pacific Ocean
4. Parliamentary constitutional republic
5. Blue (red, white, blue on the Union Jack)
6. 900000 (2018 estimate)
7. English, Fijian, Fiji Hindi
8. United Kingdom
9. President
10. Fijian dollar
11. Abel Tasman
12. One third
13. Australia
14. Tourism
15. Prime Minister
16. Methodist
17. Rugby sevens
18. October 10th
19. Left hand side
20. Suva
21. 2006
22. Rugby Union
23. .fj
24. Cyclone Mick
25. Rugby sevens

FINLAND

1. What is the capital city of Finland?
2. What are the colours on the flag of Finland?
3. Finland was controlled by which country before its independence?
4. What is the official name of Finland?
5. Between five and ten million, what is the population of Finland?
6. How many times have the Summer Olympic Games been held in Finland?
7. Hard rock/heavy metal Finnish band Lordi won the Eurovision Song Contest in what year of the 2000s?
8. What are the two official languages of Finland?
9. What side of the road do Finnish drivers drive on?
10. What letters appear at the end of a web address from Finland?
11. Which Finnish runner won a total of nine gold medals for long distance running at the Summer Olympic Games?
12. What is the national church of Finland?
13. What is the national animal of Finland?
14. What is the name of the most northerly and largest region of Finland?
15. Who is the Head of Government in Finland?
16. What is the currency of Finland?
17. What is the largest airport in Finland?
18. Which country provides the most tourists coming to Finland?

19. Which famous, legendary figure is known to live on Korvatunturi in the Lapland region of Finland?
20. From which country does Finland get the most immigrants?
21. At what age do Finnish children start school?
22. How many times has Finland hosted the Eurovision Song Contest?
23. What is the largest city in Finland?
24. On what date in December is Finland's Independence Day held?
25. What is the most popular spectator sport in Finland?

FINLAND ANSWERS

1. Helsinki
2. Blue and white
3. Russian Empire
4. Republic of Finland
5. Five (.5) million (2019 estimate)
6. Once-1952 (Helsinki)
7. 2006
8. Finnish, Swedish
9. Right hand side
10. .fi
11. Paavo Nurmi
12. Evangelical Lutheran Church of Finland
13. Brown bear
14. Lapland
15. Prime Minister
16. Euro
17. Helsinki Airport
18. Russia
19. Santa Claus
20. Russia
21. Seven
22. Once
23. Helsinki
24. December 6th
25. Ice hockey

FRANCE

1. What are the colours on the flag of France?
2. What is the official name for France?
3. How many countries share a land border with France?
4. What is the official language of France?
5. What is the name of France's National Day?
6. What is the capital of France
7. What is the currency of France?
8. Who was Emperor of France from 1804 to 1814?
9. Who was King of France at the outbreak of the French Revolution?
10. What form of government does France have?
11. Between 65 and 70 million, what is the population of France?
12. Which side of the road do French drivers drive on?
13. Who is the Head of State in France?
14. Which country provides the most tourists to France?
15. What is the most popular sport in France?
16. Which famous cycling race is held annually in France?
17. How many times have French films won the Academy Award for Best Foreign Language Film?
18. What letters appear at the end of a web address from France?
19. Which is the most visited tourist site in France?
20. How many times has France the FIFA World Cup of Football?
21. Which French designer launched the 'pret-a-porter' (ready to wear) line in the 1960s?

22. Which Frenchman suggested the revival of the Olympic Games in the 19th century?
23. Which museum in France is the most visited art museum in the world?
24. What is the largest city in France?
25. Which French heroine led France to several victories during the Hundred Years War?

FRANCE ANSWERS

1. Red, white, blue
2. French Republic
3. Seven-Belgium, Luxembourg, Germany, Andorra, Spain, Switzerland, Italy
4. French
5. Bastille Day
6. Paris
7. Euro
8. Napoleon Bonaparte
9. Louis XVI
10. Semi Presidential Republic
11. 67 million (2019 estimate)
12. Right hand side
13. President
14. Germany
15. Football
16. Tour de France
17. Nine (and three Honorary Awards before 1956)
18. .fr
19. Eiffel Tower
20. Twice-1998, 2018
21. Yves Saint Laurent
22. Baron Pierre de Coubertin
23. Louvre
24. Paris
25. Joan of Arc

GERMANY

1. What is the official name for Germany?
2. What are the colours on the flag of Germany?
3. How many countries share a border with Germany?
4. Who was the last Emperor of Germany?
5. Between 80 and 85 million, what is the population of Germany?
6. What is the currency of Germany?
7. What is the capital city of Germany?
8. In what year was the fall of the Berlin Wall, dividing East and West Berlin?
9. Who became the first female Chancellor of Germany in 2005?
10. By revenue, what is the largest company in Germany?
11. How many German laureates have been awarded Nobel Prizes?
12. Which country provides the most tourists to Germany?
13. Which side of the road do German drivers drive on?
14. Who is the Head of State in Germany?
15. What is the national alcoholic drink of Germany?
16. Who became Chancellor of Germany in 1933?
17. What is the most popular sport in Germany?
18. What letters appear at the end of a web page from Germany?
19. What is the official language of Germany?
20. How many times have German films won the Academy Award for Best Foreign Language Film?

21. How many times has Germany won the FIFA World Cup of Football?
22. What is the most visited event in Germany each year?
23. What is the largest city in Germany?
24. What is the name of the road network in Germany, known for its lack of a general speed limit?
25. In what year were East and West Germany reunified?

GERMANY ANSWERS

1. Federal Republic of Germany
2. Red, yellow, black
3. Nine-France, Belgium, Netherlands, Poland, Denmark, Czech Republic, Austria, Switzerland, Luxembourg
4. Wilhelm II
5. 83 million (2018 estimate)
6. Euro
7. Berlin
8. 1989
9. Angela Merkel
10. Volkswagen
11. 107
12. Netherlands
13. Right hand side
14. President
15. Beer
16. Adolf Hitler
17. Football
18. .de and .eu
19. German
20. Twice
21. Four times
22. Oktoberfest
23. Berlin
24. Autobahn
25. 1990

GREECE

1. What is the official name for Greece?
2. What is the capital city of Greece?
3. What colours are the flag of Greece?
4. How many countries share a land border with Greece?
5. What is the official language of Greece?
6. From which country did Greece declare its independence in 1821?
7. What form of government does Greece have?
8. Which religion is recognised in the Greek constitution?
9. Which country provides the most tourists to Greece?
10. What is the currency of Greece?
11. Between 10 and 15 million, what is the population of Greece?
12. Which countries invaded Greece in 1941?
13. In what years did Greece host the Summer Olympic Games?
14. What is the largest city in Greece?
15. Which three Greek philosophers are credited as founders of western philosophy?
16. How many times has Greece won the Eurovision Song Contest?
17. What is the most popular team sport in Greece?
18. What side of the road do drivers in Greece drive on?
19. How many times has Greece won the Academy Award for Best Foreign Language film?
20. What letters appear at the end of a web address from Greece?

21. In which sport have Greeks been the most successful at the Summer Olympic Games?
22. Which Greek musician won an Academy Award for his score in the film Chariots of Fire?
23. What is the largest island of Greece?
24. Who is the Head of State in Greece?
25. Which Greek author wrote The Odyssey and The Iliad?

GREECE ANSWERS

1. Hellenic Republic
2. Athens
3. Blue, white
4. Four-Albania, Bulgaria, Turkey, . Republic of North Macedonia
5. Greek
6. Ottoman Empire
7. Parliamentary republic
8. Eastern Orthodoxy (Greek Orthodox)
9. Republic of North Macedonia
10. Euro
11. 10(.7)million (2017 estimate)
12. Germany, Italy
13. 1896, 2004
14. Athens
15. Socrates, Plato, Aristotle
16. Once-2005
17. Football
18. Right hand side
19. None
20. .gr
21. Athletics
22. Vangelis
23. Crete
24. President
25. Homer

GUYANA

1. What is the official name of Guyana?
2. What colours are on the flag of Guyana?
3. What is the capital city of Guyana?
4. How many countries share a land border with Guyana?
5. What form of government does Guyana have?
6. Which country did Guyana gain its independence from in 1966?
7. What is the official language of Guyana?
8. Between 500000 and 900000, what is the population of Guyana?
9. What is the currency of Guyana?
10. Who is the Head of State in Guyana?
11. Which country is the main export partner of Guyana?
12. What is the dominant religious denomination of Guyana?
13. What is the largest city in Guyana?
14. What are Guyana's two main export items?
15. What is the most popular sport in Guyana?
16. Which side of the road do drivers in Guyana drive on?
17. Who is the Head of Government in Guyana?
18. Which day in May is Guyana's national holiday, Independence Day?
19. Which country is the major import partner of Guyana?
20. Where in Guyana was the mass suicide by the People's Temple cult in 1978?
21. What was the previous name for Guyana when it was a colony?
22. Guyana is part of which international cricket team?

23. What letters appear at the end of a web address from Guyana?
24. What major sporting event did Guyana co-host in 2007?
25. In which continent is Guyana?

GUYANA ANSWERS

1. Co-operative Republic of Guyana
2. Red, black, yellow, white, green
3. Georgetown
4. Three-Brazil, Venezuela, Suriname
5. Presidential, constitutional socialist republic
6. United Kingdom
7. English
8. 700000 (2016 estimate)
9. Guyanese dollar
10. President
11. United States
12. Protestant
13. Georgetown
14. Sugar, gold
15. Cricket
16. Left hand side
17. President
18. May 26th
19. Trinidad and Tobago
20. Jonestown
21. British Guiana
22. West indies
23. .gy
24. Cricket World Cup
25. South America

HAITI

1. What are the colours on the flag of Haiti?
2. What is the capital city of Haiti?
3. What is the formal name of Haiti?
4. Which family dynasty ruled Haiti from 1957 to 1986?
5. What form of government does Haiti have?
6. From which country did Haiti declare independence from in 1804?
7. What are the two official languages of Haiti?
8. Who is the Head of State in Haiti?
9. Which natural disaster in 2010 left up to 300000 people dead?
10. How many countries share a land border with Haiti?
11. What is the currency of Haiti?
12. Which country is the main export partner of Haiti?
13. Who is the Head of Government in Haiti?
14. Which country provides the most tourists to Haiti?
15. What is the dominant religious denomination in Haiti?
16. What is the largest city in Haiti?
17. What is the most popular alcoholic beverage in Haiti?
18. What is the most popular sport in Haiti?
19. Which Grammy Award winning hip-hop artist was born in Haiti?
20. Which country is the major import partner of Haiti?
21. In which two events have Haitian competitors won medals (one silver, one bronze) at the Summer Olympic Games?
22. Which side of the road do drivers in Haiti drive on?

23. Between 10 and 15 million, what is the population of Haiti?
24. Which letters appear at the end of a web address from Haiti?
25. Of which island does Haiti occupy the western side?

HAITI ANSWERS

1. Red, blue
2. Port-au-Prince
3. Republic of Haiti
4. Duvalier (Papa Doc, Baby Doc)
5. Semi-presidential republic
6. France
7. French, Haitian Creole
8. President
9. Earthquake
10. One-Dominican Republic
11. Haitian gourde
12. United States of America
13. Prime Minister
14. United States of America
15. Roman Catholic
16. Port-au-Prince
17. Rum
18. Football
19. Wyclef Jean
20. United States of America
21. Athletics, shooting
22. Right hand side
23. 10(.8) million (2016 estimate)
24. .ht
25. Hispaniola

HUNGARY

1. With which other country did Hungary join with in 1867 to form a major European power?
2. What is the capital of Hungary?
3. What are the colours on the flag of Hungary?
4. In 1956, the revolution by the Hungarians was against the rule of which country?
5. Between five and ten million, what is the population of Hungary?
6. What is the name of the patron Saint of Hungary?
7. What is the currency of Hungary?
8. What form of rule existed in Hungary from 1920 to 1946?
9. What is the official language of Hungary?
10. On which side of the road do Hungarian drivers drive?
11. Which two rivers are the main waterways of Hungary?
12. Who is the Head of State in Hungary?
13. Albert Szent-Gyorgyi a Hungarian Nobel Prize winner in Medicine, discovered which vitamin?
14. How many international airports are there in Hungary?
15. Which 19th century composer and pianist is considered Hungary's greatest composer?
16. How many Olympic titles has the Hungarian football team won?
17. What is considered the most famous Hungarian food dish?
18. What is Hungary's largest city?
19. What letters are at the end of a web address from Hungary?
20. What attracts tourists to Hungary because of their cleansing and healing properties?

21. Which country provides the most tourists to Hungary?
22. Who is the Head of Government in Hungary?
23. How many times has Hungary won the Eurovision Song Contest?
24. In which water sport is Hungary the leading medal winner at the Summer Olympic Games?
25. What is the Hungarian name for the peoples of Hungary?

HUNGARY ANSWERS

1. Austria
2. Budapest
3. Red, white and green
4. Soviet Union-USSR
5. Nine (.7) million (2019 estimate)
6. Saint Stephen
7. Forint
8. Monarchy-Kingdom of Hungary
9. Hungarian
10. Right hand side
11. Danube, Tisza
12. President
13. Vitamin C
14. Five
15. Franz Liszt
16. Three
17. Goulash
18. Budapest
19. .hu
20. Thermal baths/springs
21. Germany
22. Prime Minister
23. None
24. Water polo
25. Magyars

ICELAND

1. With which country was Iceland in a union with after the First World War?
2. What is the capital of Iceland?
3. What is the currency of Iceland?
4. In what year of the 1940s did Iceland become a republic?
5. To which country is Iceland closest geographically?
6. What is the only indigenous land mammal of Iceland?
7. Between one hundred and five hundred thousand, what is the population of Iceland?
8. What is the official language of Iceland?
9. What is the state church of Iceland?
10. How many Icelandic films have been nominated for an Academy Award?
11. Who is the most famous pop singer to come from Iceland?
12. On which side of the road to drivers in Iceland drive?
13. What are the colours on the flag of Iceland?
14. In area, what does Iceland rank in terms of islands in Europe?
15. Who is the Head of Government in Iceland?
16. What is the main form of transport in Iceland?
17. Which two renewable sources provide effectively all of Iceland's electricity?
18. In what year did Iceland make its debut at the FIFA World Cup of football?
19. Which country provides the most tourists coming to Iceland?

20. How many times has Iceland won the Eurovision Song Contest?
21. In what year did the volcano in Eyjafjallajökull erupt and cause widespread disruption to air travel in Europe?
22. What is often referred to as the national sport of Iceland?
23. Eiour Guojohnsen is Iceland's most famous athlete. At what sport did he achieve fame in?
24. What letters go at the end of a web address from Iceland?
25. What is the name of Iceland's parliament, the oldest Parliament in the world?

ICELAND ANSWERS

1. Denmark
2. Reykjavik
3. Icelandic krona
4. 1944
5. Greenland
6. Arctic fox
7. 300 000 (2019 estimate)
8. Icelandic
9. Church of Iceland
10. One-Children of Nature
11. Bjork
12. Right hand side
13. Red, white and blue
14. Second largest-after Great Britain
15. Prime Minister
16. Cars
17. Geothermal and hydropower
18. 2018
19. United States of America
20. None-2nd place twice (1999, 2009)
21. 2010
22. Handball
23. Football (Chelsea FC, Barcelona FC)
24. .is
25. Althing

INDIA

1. What are the colours on the flag of India?
2. What is the official name of India?
3. What is the capital city of India?
4. In what year of the 1940s did India gain its independence from Great Britain?
5. Who was the leader of the independence movement in India?
6. Who is the Head of State in India?
7. What is the currency of India?
8. What are the two official languages of India?
9. What is the largest religion in India?
10. What is the most popular sport in India?
11. Which side of the road do Indian drivers drive on?
12. What is the largest city in India?
13. In what year did the population of India reach 1 billion?
14. Who has been the first, and so far (2019), the only female Prime Minister of India?
15. Which famous marble mausoleum is located in the Indian city of Agra?
16. What is the popular name for Hindi Cinema from India?
17. What letters appear at the end of a web address from India?
18. What is the lowest caste in Indian society?
19. At which sport has India been the most successful at the Summer Olympic Games?
20. Who is the head of Government in India?
21. How many countries share a land border with India?

22. The Indian parliamentary system is based on which type of system?
23. Which country is the major import partner of India?
24. How many times has India hosted the Commonwealth Games?
25. On which day in August is the National holiday of Independence Day celebrated in India?

INDIA ANSWERS

1. Orange, white, green
2. Republic of India
3. New Delhi
4. 1947
5. Mahatma Gandhi
6. The President
7. Indian rupee
8. Hindi, English
9. Hinduism
10. Cricket
11. Left hand side
12. Mumbai
13. 2000
14. Indira Gandhi
15. Taj Mahal
16. Bollywood
17. .in
18. Dalit (Untouchable)
19. Field hockey
20. Prime Minister
21. Six-Pakistan, China, Bhutan, Bangladesh, Nepal, Myanmar
22. Westminster System
23. China
24. Once-2010
25. August 15th

INDONESIA

1. What is the capital city of Indonesia?
2. What are the colours on the flag of Indonesia?
3. What is the official name of Indonesia?
4. Which Indonesian island is the most populous island in the world?
5. With how many countries does Indonesia share a land border?
6. What form of government does Indonesia have?
7. From which country did Indonesia declare its independence?
8. Between 260 and 265 million, what is the population of Indonesia?
9. Who is the Head of State and the Head of Government in Indonesia?
10. What is the currency of Indonesia?
11. What side of the road do Indonesian drivers drive on?
12. Who is considered the Founding Father of Indonesia?
13. What is the official language of Indonesia?
14. In area, what is the largest island of Indonesia?
15. Being part of the Pacific Ring of Fire, what natural disasters is Indonesia susceptible to?
16. Which country provides the most tourists to Indonesia?
17. What letters are at the end of a web address from Indonesia?
18. What is the most visited tourist attraction in Indonesia?
19. What is the largest city in Indonesia?
20. What is the dominant religion of Indonesia?
21. Which two sports are the most popular in Indonesia?

22. What was the previous name of Indonesia?
23. What natural disaster claimed over 160,000 lives in Indonesia in 2004?
24. In which sport has Indonesia gained the most medals at the Summer Olympic Games?
25. Which airline is the flag carrier of Indonesia?

INDONESIA ANSWERS

1. Jakarta
2. Red and white
3. Republic of Indonesia
4. Java
5. Three-Papua New Guinea, East Timor, Malaysia
6. Constitutional Republic
7. Netherlands
8. 261 million (2016 estimate)
9. President
10. Indonesian rupiah
11. Left hand side
12. Sukarno
13. Indonesian
14. Java
15. Volcanic eruptions, earthquakes
16. China
17. .id
18. Borobudur
19. Jakarta
20. Islam (Muslim)
21. Badminton, football
22. Dutch East Indies
23. Earthquake, tsunami
24. Badminton
25. Garuda

IRAN

1. What is the capital city of Iran?
2. What is the official name of Iran?
3. What colours are on the flag of Iran?
4. How many countries share a land border with Iran?
5. What is the state religion of Iran?
6. What form of government does Iran have?
7. Who is the Head of State in Iran?
8. Between 80 and 85 million, what is the population of Iran?
9. By what other name has Iran be known as?
10. Which country is the major export partner of Iran?
11. In what year of the 1970s was an Islamic Republic set up in Iran?
12. With which country did Iran engage in war during the 1980s?
13. What is the largest city in Iran?
14. What is the official language of Iran?
15. Which countries invaded Iran in 1941?
16. Which critically endangered species of big cat now only lives in Iran?
17. What is the currency of Iran?
18. What is the most popular tourist destination in Iran?
19. What is the most popular sport in Iran?
20. How many times have Iranian films won the Academy Award for Best Foreign Language Film?
21. Which side of the road do drivers in Iran drive on?
22. Who is the Head of Government in Iran?

23. How many times has Iran won the AFC Asian Cup of football?
24. What letters appear at the end of a web address from Iran?
25. In which sport has Iran won the most medals at the Summer Olympic Games?

IRAN ANSWERS

1. Tehran
2. Islamic Republic of Iran
3. Red, white, green
4. Seven-Turkey, Iraq, Turkmenistan, Azerbaijan, Turkey, Afghanistan, Armenia, Pakistan
5. Islam
6. Khomeinist presidential Islamic republic
7. Supreme Leader
8. 82 million (2018 estimate)
9. Persia
10. China
11. 1979
12. Iraq
13. Tehran
14. Persian
15. Great Britain, Soviet Union
16. Asiatic (Iranian) cheetah
17. Rial
18. Tehran
19. Football
20. Twice
21. Right hand side
22. President
23. Three times
24. .ir
25. Wrestling

IRAQ

1. What is the official name of Iraq?
2. What is the capital city of Iraq?
3. What colours are on the flag of Iraq?
4. How many countries share a land border with Iraq?
5. What is the official religion of Iraq?
6. What form of government does Iraq have?
7. Who ruled Iraq from 1979 to 2003?
8. What are the two official languages of Iraq?
9. From which country did Iraq gain its independence in 1932?
10. Who is the Head of State in Iraq?
11. What was the name of the region that now includes modern Iraq known as in ancient times?
12. What is the largest city in Iraq?
13. What is the currency of Iraq?
14. Which country ruled Iraq up until 1918?
15. Which side of the road do drivers in Iraq drive on?
16. Which two major rivers run through Iraq?
17. Who is the Head of Government in Iraq?
18. What is the main occupation of the people of Iraq?
19. What is the most popular sport in Iraq?
20. What accounts for 99% of Iraq's revenue?
21. What form of tourism is the most popular in Iraq?
22. Which country did Iraq invade in 1990?
23. In what year did the Iraqi football team win the AFC Asian Cup?
24. What letters appear at the end of a web address from Iraq?
25. Which country is the major import partner of Iraq?

IRAQ ANSWERS

1. Republic of Iraq
2. Baghdad
3. Red, white, black, green
4. Six-Iran, Turkey, Syria, Jordan, Saudi Arabia, Kuwait
5. Islam
6. Federal parliamentary republic
7. Saddam Hussein
8. Arabic, Kurdish
9. United Kingdom
10. President
11. Mesopotamia
12. Baghdad
13. Iraqi dinar
14. Ottoman Empire
15. Right hand side
16. Tigris and Euphrates
17. Prime Minister
18. Agriculture
19. Football
20. Oil
21. Religious tourism
22. Kuwait
23. 2007
24. .iq
25. Iran

IRELAND

1. What is the Gaelic/Irish name for Ireland?
2. What is the capital of the Republic of Ireland?
3. In what year was the Easter Uprising in Ireland?
4. What are the official languages of the Republic of Ireland?
5. What is the most popular sport in the Republic of Ireland?
6. What occurred between 1845 and 1852 and claimed more than a million lives in Ireland?
7. What is the name of the river that flows through Dublin?
8. What is the currency used in the Republic of Ireland?
9. What letters are at the end of an internet address from the Republic of Ireland?
10. What side of the road do the Irish drive on?
11. In what year was the Irish Free State declared to be known as the Republic of Ireland?
12. What is the largest city in the Republic of Ireland?
13. For which brew of beer is Ireland most famous for?
14. How many counties in total are there in Ireland?
15. What is the capital of Northern Ireland?
16. Which Irish writer wrote 'Ulysses'?
17. Which has been the most successful Irish band?
18. What is considered to be the poetic name for Ireland?
19. What is the official sport of Ireland?
20. How many patron saints of Ireland are there?
21. What is the longest river in Ireland?
22. How many times has Ireland won the Eurovision Song Contest?

23. In terms of area what is the largest county in the Republic of Ireland?
24. What is the total population of Ireland-Republic and Northern Ireland combined (between five and ten million)?
25. What is the only reptile native in Ireland?

IRELAND ANSWERS

1. Eire
2. Dublin
3. 1916
4. Irish (Irish Gaelic) and English
5. Gaelic football
6. The Great Famine
7. The Liffey
8. Euro
9. .ie
10. Left hand side
11. 1949
12. Dublin
13. Guinness
14. 32
15. Belfast
16. James Joyce
17. U2
18. Emerald Isle
19. Hurling
20. Three – Saint Brigid, Saint Colmcille, Saint Patrick
21. River Shannon
22. Seven
23. County Cork
24. 6 million (2016)
25. Common lizard

ISRAEL

1. What is the official name of Israel?
2. What is the capital city of Israel?
3. What colours are on the flag of Israel?
4. How many countries share a land border with Israel?
5. What is the official language of Israel?
6. Between five and ten million, what is the population of Israel?
7. What is the dominant religion of Israel?
8. Who is the Head of State in Israel?
9. In what year of the 1940s was the independence of Israel declared?
10. What form of government does Israel have?
11. Who is the Head of Government in Israel?
12. What is the largest city in Israel?
13. What is the currency of Israel?
14. Which side of the road do drivers in Israel drive on?
15. What is the holiest day of the year in Judaism?
16. Who is regarded as the founder of modern Israel and was its first Prime Minister?
17. Under Israeli law, how many countries are enemy countries?
18. How many Israelis have won a Nobel Prize?
19. Which country provides the most tourists to Israel?
20. What are the two most popular spectator sports in Israel?
21. What letters are at the end of a web address from Israel?
22. What symbol is on the flag of Israel?
23. What is the most visited site in Israel?
24. Which country is Israeli's biggest export partner?
25. Who was Israel's only female Prime Minister (to date)?

ISRAEL ANSWERS

1. State of Israel
2. Tel Aviv (Jerusalem-limited recognition)
3. Blue, white
4. Four-Lebanon, Egypt, Jordan, Syria + Palestinian territories of West Bank and Gaza Strip
5. Hebrew
6. Nine million (2019 estimate)
7. Jewish
8. President
9. 1948
10. Parliamentary republic
11. Prime Minister
12. Jerusalem
13. New shekel
14. Right hand side
15. Yom Kippur
16. David Ben-Gurion
17. Seven-Saudi Arabia, Syria, Lebanon, Iraq, Iran, Sudan, Yemen
18. Twelve
19. United States
20. Football, basketball
21. .il
22. Star of David
23. Western (Wailing) Wall
24. United States
25. Golda Meir

ITALY

1. What are the colours on the flag of Italy?
2. Between 60 and 65 million, what is the population of Italy?
3. What is the official name of Italy?
4. With how many countries/sovereign states does Italy share a border?
5. Who, with the Black shirts, led a coup in Rome in 1922?
6. In what year of the 1940s did Italy become a Republic?
7. Who is the Head of Government in Italy?
8. What is the capital city of Italy?
9. What is the main religion in Italy
10. Which Italian sculptor created the Statue of David?
11. What is the most popular sport in Italy?
12. How many times have Italian films won the Academy Award for Best Foreign Language Film?
13. How many times has Italy won the Eurovision Song Contest?
14. What is the currency of Italy?
15. On what side of the road do Italian drivers drive?
16. What is the name of the top fight football competition in Italy called?
17. How many times has Italy hosted the Winter Olympics?
18. Which three Italian cities are the main fashion capitals?
19. Which Italian songwriter, DJ and producer is considered the 'Father of Disco'?
20. What are the letters that go at the end of a web address from Italy?

21. Which mountain range runs along the length of the Italian peninsula?
22. From which country does Italy receive the most tourists?
23. In which Italian city was pizza invented?
24. What is the largest city in Italy?
25. What is the official language of Italy?

ITALY ANSWERS

1. Red, white and green
2. 60 million (2017 estimate)
3. Italian Republic
4. Six-France, Switzerland, San Marino, Vatican City, Austria, Slovenia
5. Benito Mussolini
6. 1946
7. Prime Minister
8. Rome
9. Roman Catholic
10. Michelangelo
11. Football
12. 14 times
13. Twice-1964, 1990
14. Euro
15. Right hand side
16. Serie A
17. Twice-1956, 2006
18. Milan, Florence, Rome
19. Giorgio Moroder
20. .it
21. Apennine Mountains
22. Germany
23. Naples
24. Rome
25. Italian

JAMAICA

1. What is the capital of Jamaica?
2. Which colours are on the flag of Jamaica?
3. From which country did Jamaica gain its independence in 1962?
4. Who is the head of state in Jamaica?
5. Which two indigenous peoples originally inhabited Jamaica?
6. On which side of the road do Jamaican drivers drive?
7. Who first claimed Jamaica for Spain in 1494?
8. What is the official language of Jamaica?
9. Who is the most famous reggae artist to come from Jamaica?
10. What are the two main industries of the Jamaican economy?
11. How many lighthouses operate in Jamaica?
12. In what year did the Jamaican bobsled team first participate at the Winter Olympics?
13. What is the most well-known Jamaican form of cuisine?
14. What is the main form of religion in Jamaica?
15. At which venue is Test cricket played in Jamaica?
16. What is the largest city in Jamaica?
17. Which future American President spent his honeymoon in Jamaica?
18. How many of Jamaica's eight species of native snakes are venomous?
19. What is the currency of Jamaica?

20. What letters appear at the end of a website address from Jamaica?
21. Who has been the most successful Jamaican athlete at the Summer Olympic Games?
22. How many times has Jamaica qualified for the FIFA World Cup of Football?
23. What is Jamaica's most popular women's sport?
24. In area, what is Jamaica's rank in the Caribbean?
25. Between one and five million, what is the population of Jamaica?

JAMAICA ANSWERS

1. Kingston
2. Black, yellow, green
3. United Kingdom
4. Queen Elizabeth II (British monarch)
5. Arawak, Taino
6. Left hand side
7. Christopher Columbus
8. English
9. Bob Marley
10. Tourism, mining
11. Nine
12. 1988
13. Jamaican jerk spice
14. Protestant
15. Sabina Park
16. Kingston
17. John F Kennedy
18. None
19. Jamaican dollar
20. .jm
21. Usain Bolt
22. Once (1998)
23. Netball
24. Third
25. 3 million (2017 estimate)

JAPAN

1. How many main islands make up 97% of Japan's land area?
2. What are the colours on the flag of Japan?
3. What is the capital city of Japan?
4. Between 125 and 130 million, what is the population of Japan?
5. What is the official language of Japan?
6. Who is the Head of Government in Japan?
7. What is the Japanese name for Japan?
8. What was the name of the ruling class of warriors in Japan during feudal times?
9. What is the currency of Japan?
10. Which country provides the most tourists to Japan?
11. What is the name of the form of animation associated with Japan called?
12. How many times has Japan won the Academy Award for Best Foreign Language Film?
13. What is the most popular spectator sport in Japan?
14. Who is the Head of State in Japan?
15. On which side of the road do Japanese drivers drive?
16. What is the highest mountain in Japan?
17. What letters appear at the end of a web address from Japan?
18. What is the largest city in Japan?
19. What is traditionally considered to be Japan's national sport?
20. How many times has Japan hosted the Winter Olympics?

21. National Foundation Day celebrates the mythological foundation of Japan is held on which day in February?
22. What is the national beverage of Japan?
23. What name are Japanese comics known by?
24. What is the largest religion in Japan?
25. Which airline is the flag carrier of Japan?

JAPAN ANSWERS

1. Four
2. Red and white
3. Tokyo
4. 126 million (2019 census)
5. Japanese
6. Prime Minister
7. Nippon
8. Samurai
9. Yen
10. China
11. Anime
12. Four times
13. Baseball
14. The Emperor
15. Left hand side
16. Mount Fuji
17. .jp
18. Tokyo
19. Sumo wrestling
20. Twice-1972, 1998
21. February 11th
22. Sake
23. Manga
24. Shinto
25. Japan Airlines

JORDAN

1. What is the official name of Jordan?
2. What is the capital city of Jordan?
3. What colours are on the flag of Jordan?
4. How many countries share a land border with Jordan?
5. What is the official religion of Jordan?
6. What form of government does Jordan have?
7. From which country did gain its independence in 1946?
8. Between 10 and 15million, what is the population of Jordan?
9. What is the official language of Jordan?
10. Who is the Head of State in Jordan?
11. What is the largest city in Jordan?
12. What was the slightly longer name for Jordan before its independence?
13. What is the currency of Jordan?
14. Which body of water located in Jordan is the lowest point and saltiest on Earth?
15. With which other country did Jordan sign a peace treaty in 1994?
16. Who is the Head of Government in Jordan?
17. Which country provides the most tourists to Jordan?
18. Which historical city, carved in a mountain, is located in Jordan?
19. What is the most popular sport in Jordan?
20. Which side of the road do drivers in Jordan drive on?
21. What is the national food dish of Jordan?

22. How many times has a film from Jordan been nominated for an Academy Award for Best Foreign Language Film?
23. Which country is Jordan's major export partner?
24. What letters appear at the end of a web address from Jordan?
25. Which empire ruled Jordan for over four centuries, ending during World War One?

JORDAN ANSWERS

1. Hashemite Kingdom of Jordan
2. Amman
3. Red, white, black, green
4. Five-Saudi Arabia, Syria, Israel, Palestine(West Bank), Iraq
5. Islam
6. Parliamentary constitutional monarchy
7. United Kingdom
8. 10(.4) million (2019 estimate)
9. Arabic
10. Monarch
11. Amman
12. Transjordan
13. Jordanian dinar
14. Dead Sea
15. Israel
16. Prime Minister
17. Saudi Arabia
18. Petra
19. Football
20. Right hand side
21. Mansaf-lamb cooked in fermented dry yoghurt
22. Once-2016
23. Iraq
24. .jo
25. Ottoman Empire

KENYA

1. What are the colours on the flag of Kenya?
2. What is the official name of Kenya?
3. What is the capital city of Kenya?
4. What are the two official languages of Kenya?
5. How many countries share a land border with Kenya?
6. Between 45 and 50 million, what is the population of Kenya?
7. From which country did Kenya gain its independence in 1963?
8. What form of government does Kenya have?
9. What is Kenya named after?
10. What is the currency of Kenya?
11. Who is the Head of State and Head of Government in Kenya?
12. Which cash crop is Kenya's largest export?
13. What are the main tourist attractions in Kenya?
14. Which side of the road do drivers in Kenya drive on?
15. What is the national language of Kenya?
16. Which country is the major export partner of Kenya?
17. At which athletic events have Kenyan runners been dominant at the Summer Olympic Games?
18. What is the dominant religious denomination in Kenya?
19. What is the largest city in Kenya?
20. What are the letters that are at the end of a web address from Kenya?
21. Jomo Kenyatta was the first what of Kenya?
22. Which animal features on the coat of arms of Kenya?

23. What is Kenya's best place finish at the ICC World Cup of Cricket?
24. Which country provides the most tourists to Kenya?
25. Which armed forces fought in Kenya during World War Two?

KENYA ANSWERS

1. Red, black, white, green
2. Republic of Kenya
3. Nairobi
4. English, Swahili
5. Five-Uganda, South Sudan, Somalia, Tanzania, Ethiopia
6. 49 million (2019 estimate)
7. United Kingdom
8. Presidential constitutional republic
9. Mount Kenya
10. Kenyan shilling
11. President
12. Tea
13. Photo safaris
14. Left hand side
15. Swahili
16. Uganda
17. Middle and long distance running
18. Protestant
19. Nairobi
20. .ke
21. President
22. Two lions
23. Semi-finals 2003
24. Germany
25. Allied and Italian

KOREA

1. What are the two sovereign states that comprise Korea?
2. Which two countries share a land border with Korea?
3. During which years was the Korean War fought?
4. What is the official language of Korea?
5. In what year was Korea divided into north and south?
6. What are the official names of the two divided states of Korea?
7. What are the two capital cities of the divided states?
8. Between 75 and 80 million, what is the combined population of the two divided Korean states?
9. What colours are similar to the two flags of the Korean states?
10. Which country ruled Korea before independence?
11. What is the largest city in Korea?
12. What is regarded as Korea's most famous sport?
13. What side of the road do Korean drivers drive on?
14. What is the currency of both states of Korea?
15. What is the most popular sport in both states of Korea?
16. Which family dynasty has ruled North Korea since independence?
17. In which sport did Korea compete as a unified team at the 2018 Winter Olympics?
18. What letters are at the end of a web address sent from the two separate states of Korea?
19. Which two countries occupied the north and south of Korea after World War II?
20. Which country provides the most tourists to South Korea?

21. Which line of latitude is famous as the division between the Korean states?
22. What precipitated the start of the Korean War?
23. What is unusual about the end of the Korean War?
24. What types of chopsticks are used in eating Korean food?
25. What colour is only on one of the flags of the two Korean states?

KOREA ANSWERS

1. North Korea, South Korea
2. Russia, China
3. 1950-1953
4. Korean
5. 1948
6. Democratic People's Republic of Korea (North), Republic of Korea (South)
7. Pyongyang (North), Seoul (South)
8. 77 million (2017 estimate)
9. Red, white, blue
10. Japan
11. Seoul
12. Taekwondo
13. Right hand side
14. North Korean won, South Korean won
15. Football
16. Kim Dynasty
17. Women's ice hockey
18. .kp (North) .kr (South)
19. Soviet Union (North), United States (South)
20. China
21. 38th parallel
22. North Korea invaded South Korea
23. No peace treaty was signed, only an armistice
24. Metal chopsticks
25. Black-South Korea

LATVIA

1. What is the capital city of Latvia?
2. What is the official name of Latvia?
3. What colours are on the flag of Latvia?
4. How many countries share a land border with Latvia?
5. What is the collective name of the countries of Latvia, Lithuania and Estonia?
6. From which country did Latvia gain its independence in 1991?
7. What is the official language of Latvia?
8. Which country invaded Latvia in 1941?
9. What form of government does Latvia have?
10. What is the currency of Latvia?
11. Between one and five million, what is the population of Latvia?
12. Who is the Head of State in Latvia?
13. What is the dominant religious denomination in Latvia?
14. What is the largest city in Latvia?
15. Which side of the road do drivers in Latvia drive on?
16. What is the most popular sport in Latvia?
17. What is the national flower of Latvia?
18. How many times has Latvia won the Eurovision Song Contest?
19. From which country does Latvia import all its natural gas?
20. In which sport has Latvia won 2 of its 3 gold medals at the Summer Olympic Games?
21. What letters appear at the end of a web address from Latvia?

22. Who is the Head of Government in Latvia?
23. Which airline is the flag carrier of Latvia?
24. In which sport has Latvia won its only gold medal (as of 2018) at the Winter Olympics?
25. Jelena Ostapenko became the first Latvian tennis player to win which Grand Slam title?

LATVIA ANSWERS

1. Riga
2. Republic of Latvia
3. Red, white
4. Four-Lithuania, Estonia, Russia, Belarus
5. Baltic States
6. Soviet Union
7. Latvian
8. Germany
9. Parliamentary constitutional republic
10. Euro
11. One(.9) million (2018 estimate)
12. President
13. Lutheran
14. Riga
15. Right hand side
16. Ice hockey
17. Daisy
18. Once-2002
19. Russia
20. Cycling
21. .lv
22. Prime Minister
23. Air Baltic
24. Bobsleigh (four man)
25. French Open 2017

LEBANON

1. What is the formal name of Lebanon?
2. What is the capital city of Lebanon?
3. What colours are on the flag of Lebanon?
4. How many countries share a land border with Lebanon?
5. Between five and ten million, what is the population of Lebanon?
6. What form of government does Lebanon have?
7. What is the official language of Lebanon?
8. From which country did Lebanon gain its independence?
9. Which country is the major import partner of Lebanon?
10. Who is the Head of State in Lebanon?
11. Claiming an estimated 120,000 fatalities, the Lebanese Civil War lasted between what years?
12. What is the currency of Lebanon?
13. What is the largest city in Lebanon?
14. What is the main export commodity of Lebanon?
15. Who is the Head of Government in Lebanon?
16. Which country provides the most tourists to Lebanon?
17. What are the two most popular sports in Lebanon?
18. Which side of the road do drivers in Lebanon drive on?
19. Which country occupied Lebanon until 2005?
20. How many medals in total has Lebanon won at the Summer Olympic Games?
21. Which country is Lebanon's major export partner?
22. What letters are at the end of a web address from Lebanon?
23. What is the national emblem of Lebanon?

24. Which rugby league player is considered the greatest from Lebanon to play the game, holding the record for the greatest point-scorer in Australian NRL history?
25. By convention, what religion must the President of Lebanon always be?

LEBANON ANSWERS

1. Lebanese Republic
2. Beirut
3. Red, white, green
4. Two-Syria, Israel
5. Six million (2016 estimate)
6. Parliamentary multi-confessionalist republic
7. Arabic
8. France
9. China
10. President
11. 1975-1990
12. Lebanese Pound
13. Beirut
14. Gold
15. Prime Minister
16. Syria
17. Basketball, football
18. Right hand side
19. Syria
20. Four-2 silver, 2 bronze
21. China
22. .lb
23. Cedar tree
24. Hazem El Masri
25. Maronite Christian

LIBYA

1. What is the official name of Libya?
2. What is the capital city of Libya?
3. What colours are on the flag of Libya?
4. How many countries share a land border with Libya?
5. What is the official language of Libya?
6. Which military leader ruled Libya from 1969 to 2011?
7. What is the main religion of Libya?
8. Between five and ten million, what is the population of Libya?
9. What form of government does Libya have (as of 2019)?
10. From which country did Libya gain its independence in 1947?
11. What is the major export of Libya?
12. What is the largest city in Libya?
13. Who is the Head of State in Libya?
14. What is the most popular sport in Libya?
15. What is the currency of Libya?
16. Which country is the major export partner of Libya?
17. What are the main tourist attractions of Libya?
18. Which two foods are the staple foods of Libya?
19. Which country is the major import partner of Libya?
20. Which side of the road do drivers in Libya drive on?
21. How many medals has Libya won at the Summer Olympic Games?
22. What letters appear at the end of a web address from Libya?

23. What is the best result Libya has had at the Africa Cup of Nations football tournament?
24. Which desert covers 92% of Libyan territory?
25. Who has been Libya's only monarch?

LIBYA ANSWERS

1. State of Libya
2. Tripoli
3. Red, black, green
4. Six-Egypt, Sudan, Tunisia, Algeria, Niger, Chad
5. Arabic
6. Colonel Muammar Gaddafi
7. Islam
8. Six million (2016 estimate)
9. Government of National Accord
10. Italy
11. Oil
12. Tripoli
13. Chairman of the Presidential Council
14. Football
15. Libyan dinar
16. Italy
17. Ancient Roman sites
18. Pasta, rice
19. China
20. Right hand side
21. None
22. .ly
23. Runners-up 2012
24. Sahara Desert
25. Idris I (1951-1969)

LIECHTENSTEIN

1. What is the formal name of Liechtenstein?
2. What is the capital city of Liechtenstein?
3. How many countries share a land border with Liechtenstein?
4. What are the colours on the flag of Liechtenstein?
5. What is the official language of Liechtenstein?
6. What form of government does Liechtenstein have?
7. Between 35000 and 40000, what is the population of Liechtenstein?
8. What is the state religion of Liechtenstein?
9. Who is the Head of State in Liechtenstein?
10. What was Liechtenstein's role in World War Two?
11. Which river is partly a border between Liechtenstein and Switzerland?
12. What is the currency of Liechtenstein?
13. What is the biggest municipality (city) in Liechtenstein?
14. What is the most popular sport in Liechtenstein?
15. Which side of the road do drivers in Liechtenstein drive on?
16. In which league do Liechtenstein football teams play?
17. What is unique about the Liechtenstein military?
18. Which two countries provide the most tourists to Liechtenstein?
19. Which group of countries is the major export partner of Liechtenstein?
20. At which sport in the Winter Olympics has Liechtenstein won all its medals?
21. What letters appear at the end of a web address from Liechtenstein?

22. How many times has Liechtenstein participated at the Eurovision Song Contest?
23. How many television channels are there in Liechtenstein?
24. How many airports are there in Liechtenstein?
25. Population wise, how many other European countries have smaller populations than Liechtenstein?

LIECHTENSTEIN ANSWERS

1. Principality of Liechtenstein
2. Vaduz
3. Two-Switzerland, Austria
4. Red, blue, gold
5. German
6. Parliamentary constitutional monarchy
7. 38 thousand (2017 estimate)
8. Roman Catholic
9. Monarch
10. Neutral
11. Rhine River
12. Swiss franc
13. Schaan
14. Football
15. Right hand side
16. Swiss leagues
17. There is no military
18. Germany, Switzerland
19. European Union
20. Alpine skiing
21. .li
22. None
23. One
24. None-nearest is in Zurich
25. Three-Monaco, Vatican City, San Marino

LITHUANIA

1. What is the capital city of Lithuania?
2. What colours are on the flag of Lithuania?
3. What is the formal name of Lithuania?
4. How many countries share a land border with Lithuania?
5. Between one and five million, what is the population of Lithuania?
6. What form of government does Lithuania have?
7. In what year of the 1910s did Lithuania declare its independence?
8. Which two countries occupied Lithuania during World War II?
9. Who is the Head of State in Lithuania?
10. What is the official language of Lithuania?
11. What is the collective name for the countries Latvia, Lithuania and Estonia?
12. What is the currency of Lithuania?
13. What is the national bird of Lithuania?
14. What is the largest city in Lithuania?
15. Who is the Head of Government in Lithuania?
16. Which country is the major export partner of Lithuania?
17. Which country provides the most tourists to Lithuania?
18. What is the dominant religious denomination in Lithuania?
19. What is the most popular sport in Lithuania?
20. Which side of the road do drivers in Lithuania drive on?
21. On which day in February is the national holiday, Lithuanian State Reestablishment Day held?

22. In which sport has Lithuania won the most medals at the Summer Olympic Games?
23. Which country is the major import partner of Lithuania?
24. What is the best result Lithuania has had at the Eurovision Song Contest?
25. What letters appear at the end of a web address from Lithuania?

LITHUANIA ANSWERS

1. Vilnius
2. Yellow, green, red
3. Republic of Lithuania
4. Three-Poland, Latvia, Belarus (Kaliningrad Oblast-Russian enclave)
5. Two (.7) million (2019 estimate)
6. Semi-presidential republic
7. 1918
8. Soviet Union, Germany
9. President
10. Lithuanian
11. Baltic States
12. Euro
13. White stork
14. Vilnius
15. Prime Minister
16. Russia
17. Germany
18. Roman Catholic
19. Basketball
20. Right hand side
21. February 16th
22. Athletics
23. Russia
24. 6th-2006
25. .lt

LUXEMBOURG

1. Wat is the official name for Luxembourg?
2. What is the capital city of Luxembourg?
3. What are the colours on the flag of Luxembourg?
4. How many countries share a land border with Luxembourg?
5. What are the three official languages of Luxembourg?
6. What form of government is there in Luxembourg?
7. Which country invaded Luxembourg in World War One?
8. As well as being the capital city, what other distinction does the capital of Luxembourg have in Europe?
9. What is the currency of Luxembourg?
10. From which country did Luxembourg end its union in 1890?
11. Who is the Head of Government in Luxembourg?
12. What side of the road do drivers in Luxembourg drive on?
13. What is the main religious denomination in Luxembourg?
14. Luxembourg's education system is trilingual-what language is learnt first?
15. What is the most popular sport in Luxembourg?
16. What letters appear at the end of a web address from Luxembourg?
17. How many Gold medals has Luxembourg won at the Summer Olympic Games?
18. Which country has provided the most immigrants to Luxembourg?
19. What is the largest city in Luxembourg?
20. Which country provides the most tourists to Luxembourg?
21. How many times has Luxembourg won the Eurovision Song Contest?

22. Who is the Head of State in Luxembourg?
23. Where was the exiled government of Luxembourg based during the occupation in World War Two?
24. What is a person from Luxembourg referred to as?
25. How many universities are there in Luxembourg?

LUXEMBOURG ANSWERS

1. Grand Duchy of Luxembourg
2. Luxembourg City
3. Red, white, blue
4. Three-Belgium, France, Germany
5. French, German, Luxembourgish
6. Parliamentary Constitutional Monarchy
7. Germany
8. One of three official capital cities of the European Union
9. Euro
10. Netherlands
11. Prime Minister
12. Right hand side
13. Roman Catholic
14. German
15. Football
16. .lu
17. One-1500m 1952
18. Portugal
19. Luxembourg City
20. Belgium
21. Five times
22. Grand Duke
23. England-London
24. Luxembourger
25. One

MALAYSIA

1. What is the capital city of Malaysia?
2. What is the official name of Malaysia?
3. What colours are on the flag of Malaysia?
4. Between 30 and 35 million, what is the population of Malaysia?
5. How many countries share a land border with Malaysia?
6. What is the official language of Malaysia?
7. From which country did Malaysia gain its independence?
8. What form of government does Malaysia have?
9. Who is the Head of State in Malaysia?
10. What is the currency of Malaysia?
11. What is the largest city in Malaysia?
12. In what year of the 1960s was the name Malaysia adopted as the name of the country?
13. What is the dominant religion in Malaysia?
14. What is the penalty for such crimes as kidnapping, murder, drug trafficking and terrorism in Malaysia?
15. Which sea separates the two parts of Malaysia?
16. What is Malaysia's biggest export?
17. Which side of the road do drivers in Malaysia drive on?
18. On which day in August is the national holiday Independence Day observed?
19. What is the most popular sport in Malaysia?
20. Which country provides the most tourists to Malaysia?
21. Located in Malaysia, what are the tallest twin towers in the world?

22. What letters appear at the end of a web address from Malaysia?
23. What is the national airline of Malaysia?
24. Which major sporting event was hosted by Malaysia in 1998?
25. Which country is the major export partner of Malaysia?

MALAYSIA ANSWERS

1. Kuala Lumpur
2. Malaysia
3. Red, white, blue, yellow
4. 32 million (2017 estimate)
5. Three-Thailand, [Brunei, Indonesia (East Malaysia)]
6. Malay
7. United Kingdom
8. Federal parliamentary constitutional republic
9. Monarch
10. Ringgit
11. Kuala Lumpur
12. 1963
13. Islam
14. Death penalty
15. South China Sea
16. Electronic integrated circuits
17. Left hand side
18. August 31st
19. Football
20. Singapore
21. Petronas Twin Towers
22. .my
23. Malaysia Airlines
24. Commonwealth Games
25. China

MALDIVES

1. What is the official name of the Maldives?
2. What colours are on the flag of the Maldives?
3. What is the capital city of the Maldives?
4. How many countries share a land border with the Maldives?
5. Between 100000 and 500000, what is the population of the Maldives?
6. What form of government does the Maldives have?
7. What is the official language of the Maldives?
8. From which country did the Maldives gain its independence in 1965?
9. What is the official religion of the Maldives?
10. Who is the Head of State in the Maldives?
11. What natural disaster in late 2004 devastated large parts of the Maldives?
12. What is the currency of the Maldives?
13. Which country is the Maldives main export trading partner?
14. Which side of the road do drivers in the Maldives drive on?
15. What is the largest industry in the Maldives?
16. What is the main ingredient in the cuisine of the Maldives?
17. Who is the Head of Government in the Maldives?
18. Which country provides the most tourists to the Maldives?
19. What is the main environmental issue facing the Maldives in the long term?
20. What letters are at the end of a web address from the Maldives?
21. Which country is the main import trading partner of the Maldives?

22. The use of what is illegal for fishing in the Maldives?
23. What is the largest city in the Maldives?
24. What are the three ways to travel between the islands in the Maldives?
25. What are the islands of the Maldives made from?

MALDIVES ANSWERS

1. Republic of Maldives
2. Red, green white
3. Male
4. None
5. 390000 (2018 estimate)
6. Presidential republic
7. Dhivehi
8. United Kingdom
9. Islam
10. President
11. Tsunami
12. Maldivian rufiyaa
13. Sri Lanka
14. Left hand side
15. Tourism
16. Fish
17. President
18. China
19. Rising sea levels
20. .mv
21. China
22. Fishing nets
23. Male
24. Domestic flights, seaplane, boat
25. Coral

MALTA

1. What is the official name of Malta?
2. What is the capital city of Malta?
3. In which sea is Malta located?
4. What form of government does Malta have?
5. What colours are on the flag of Malta?
6. Between 100000 and 500000, what is the population of Malta?
7. What are the two official languages of Malta?
8. Who is the Head of State in Malta?
9. From which country did Malta gain its independence in 1964?
10. What was Malta awarded because of its heroism during World War Two?
11. Which country is Malta's major export partner?
12. Which country provides the most tourists to Malta?
13. What is the currency of Malta?
14. Who is the Head of Government in Malta?
15. What is the dominant religious denomination of Malta?
16. What symbol is on the flag of Malta?
17. What is the most popular sport in Malta?
18. What day in September is the national holiday in Malta, Independence Day?
19. Which side of the road do drivers in Malta drive on?
20. What is the largest city in Malta?
21. Which country is Malta's major import partner?
22. What is the main source of Malta's electricity production?

23. How many times has Malta been runner-up in the Eurovision Song Contest?
24. What letters appear at the end of a web address from Malta?
25. Malta was the venue between which two world leaders in 1989 which signalled the end of the Cold War?

MALTA ANSWERS

1. Republic of Malta
2. Valletta
3. Mediterranean Sea
4. Parliamentary constitutional republic
5. Red, white
6. 475000 (2018 estimate)
7. Maltese, English
8. President
9. United Kingdom
10. George Cross
11. Germany
12. United Kingdom
13. Euro
14. Prime Minister
15. Roman Catholic
16. George Cross
17. Football
18. September 21st
19. Left hand side
20. Valletta
21. Italy
22. Oil
23. Twice-2002, 2005
24. .mt
25. George HW Bush, Mikhail Gorbachev

MEXICO

1. What is the official name for Mexico?
2. What is the capital city of Mexico?
3. What are the colours on the flag of Mexico?
4. What is the national language of Mexico?
5. How many countries share a land border with Mexico?
6. From which country did Mexico declare its independence in 1810?
7. What form of government does Mexico have?
8. What is the currency of Mexico?
9. Between 125 and 130 million, what is the population of Mexico?
10. Which empire ruled Mexico before the European conquest?
11. Who is both Head of State and Head of Government in Mexico?
12. On which side of the road do Mexican drivers drive?
13. What is the largest city in Mexico?
14. Which country provides the most tourists to Mexico?
15. Which country is the major export partner of Mexico?
16. What day in September is commemorated as Mexico's Independence Day?
17. What is the most popular sport in Mexico?
18. Who is the only Mexican actor to win an Academy Award in acting?
19. What letters are at the end of a web address from Mexico?
20. Which Mexican city hosted the 1968 Summer Olympic Games?
21. What is the main religion of Mexico?

22. Which cereal grain was domesticated by Mexicans over 10000 years ago?

23. How many times has Mexico hosted the FIFA World Cup of Football?

24. Which Mexican city, once famous for its beach resorts, is now Mexico's deadliest city?

25. Which country is Mexico's largest import partner?

Done

MEXICO ANSWERS

1. United Mexican States
2. Mexico City
3. Red, white, green
4. Spanish
5. Three-United States, Guatemala, Belize
6. Spain
7. Federal Presidential Constitutional Republic
8. Peso
9. 126 million (2019 estimate)
10. Aztec Empire
11. President
12. Right hand side
13. Mexico City
14. United States of America
15. United States of America
16. September 16th
17. Football
18. Anthony Quinn-twice
19. .mx
20. Mexico City
21. Roman Catholicism
22. Corn
23. Twice-1970, 1986
24. Acapulco
25. United States of America

MONACO

1. What is the official name of Monaco?
2. What is the official language of Monaco?
3. Which political group has ruled Monaco, virtually uninterrupted, since 1297?
4. What famous sporting event is held in Monaco every year?
5. Who is the Head of State in Monaco?
6. What is the form of government in Monaco?
7. On what side of the road do drivers drive on in Monaco?
8. What is the form of currency used in Monaco?
9. A famous wedding occurred between which two people in Monaco in the 1950s?
10. In terms of area, what rank does Monaco have in the world?
11. How much tax is paid by the citizens of Monaco?
12. What is the name of the famous casino located in Monaco?
13. What is the full name of the football team that plays in Ligue 1 of the French competition?
14. What is the official religion of Monaco?
15. Between 35000 and 40000, what is the population of Monaco?
16. In what year of the 20th century was the first Monte Carlo Grand Prix held?
17. How many times has the Monaco football team won the Ligue 1 title?
18. What are the colours on the flag of Monaco?
19. What letters are at the end of an internet address from Monaco?

20. What is considered the traditional national language of Monaco?
21. How many state operated schools are there in total in Monaco?
22. What is the title of the Head of Government in Monaco?
23. Which country is responsible for the defence of Monaco?
24. How many fatalities have there been at the Monaco Grand Prix?
25. How many countries does the Monaco Marathon pass through?

MONACO ANSWERS

1. Principality of Monaco
2. French
3. House of Grimaldi
4. Monaco Grand Prix
5. Monarch-Prince Albert II
6. Constitutional Monarchy
7. Right hand side
8. Euro
9. Prince Rainier and Grace Kelly
10. Second smallest in the world
11. None
12. Monte Carlo
13. AS Monaco FC
14. Roman Catholic
15. 38 000 (2016 census)
16. 1929
17. Eight times
18. Red and white
19. .mc
20. Monégasque
21. Ten (+ one university)
22. Minister of State
23. France
24. One
25. Three (Monaco, France, Italy)

MOROCCO

1. What is the official name of Morocco?
2. What is the capital city of Morocco?
3. What are the colours on the flag of Morocco?
4. How many countries share a land border with Morocco?
5. In what year of the 1950s did Morocco gain its independence?
6. What are the two official languages of Morocco?
7. What is the predominant religion of Morocco?
8. What form of government does Morocco have?
9. Between 35 and 40 million, what is the population of Morocco?
10. What is the main export of Morocco?
11. What is the largest city in Morocco?
12. Which country is the major export partner of Morocco?
13. Which two countries provide the most tourists to Morocco?
14. What is the currency of Morocco?
15. Which country do most migrants to Morocco come from?
16. Which side of the road do drivers in Morocco drive on?
17. Where did Morocco finish in its only appearance at the Eurovision Song Contest in 1980?
18. What is the most commonly eaten meat in Morocco?
19. What is the most popular sport in Morocco?
20. What letters appear at the end of a web address from Morocco?
21. What is the most popular drink in Morocco?
22. In which sport has Morocco won all its gold medals at the Summer Olympic Games?

23. Who is considered the founder of Morocco?
24. Who is the Head of Government in Morocco?
25. Which two countries had Morocco as protectorates until its independence?

MOROCCO ANSWERS

1. Kingdom of Morocco
2. Rabat
3. Red, green
4. Two-Algeria, Mauritania
5. 1956
6. Arabic, Berber
7. Islam
8. Parliamentary constitutional monarchy
9. 35(.7) million (2017 census)
10. Electric wire
11. Casablanca
12. Spain
13. France, Spain
14. Moroccan dirham
15. France
16. Right hand side
17. Second last
18. Beef
19. Football
20. .ma
21. Green tea
22. Athletics
23. Idris I
24. Prime Minister
25. France, Spain

MOZAMBIQUE

1. What colours are on the flag of Mozambique?
2. What is the official name of Mozambique?
3. How many countries share a land border with Mozambique?
4. In which continent is Mozambique?
5. What is the capital city of Mozambique?
6. What is the official language of Mozambique?
7. What form of government does Mozambique have?
8. From which country did Mozambique gain its independence in 1975?
9. Between 25 and 30 million, what is the population of Mozambique?
10. Which river runs through Mozambique?
11. Which country is the major export partner of Mozambique?
12. What is the currency of Mozambique?
13. Which country provides the most tourists to Mozambique?
14. What is the main export commodity of Mozambique?
15. What is the largest city in Mozambique?
16. Who is the Head of State in Mozambique?
17. Which country is the largest import partner of Mozambique?
18. What is the most popular sport in Mozambique?
19. What is the dominant religious denomination in Mozambique?
20. What day in June is the national holiday National Independence Day held in Mozambique?
21. Which side of the road do drivers in Mozambique drive on?
22. Who is the Head of Government in Mozambique?

23. In which sport has Mozambique won its two medals-gold and bronze, at the Summer Olympic Games?
24. Which country is the major export partner of Mozambique?
25. What letters appear at the end of a web address from Mozambique?

MOZAMBIQUE ANSWERS

1. Green, black, yellow, red
2. Republic of Mozambique
3. Six-South Africa, Zimbabwe, Tanzania, Malawi, Zambia, Eswatini (Swaziland)
4. Africa
5. Maputo
6. Portuguese
7. Dominant party semi-presidential constitutional republic
8. Portugal
9. 28 million (2016 estimate)
10. Zambezi River
11. South Africa
12. Mozambican metical
13. South Africa
14. Aluminium
15. Matola
16. President
17. South Africa
18. Football
19. Roman Catholic
20. June 25th
21. Left hand side
22. President
23. Athletics-women's 800m
24. South Africa
25. .mz

MYANMAR

1. What is the former name of Myanmar, still used at times?
2. In which continent is Myanmar?
3. What is the official name of Myanmar?
4. What is the capital city of Myanmar?
5. How many countries share a land border with Myanmar?
6. What colours are on the flag of Myanmar?
7. Between 50 and 55 million, what is the population of Myanmar?
8. From which country was Myanmar granted independence in 1948?
9. What form of government does Myanmar have?
10. Whose political party gained the most votes in the election in 2015?
11. What is the official language of Myanmar?
12. Who is the Head of State in Myanmar?
13. What is the dominant religion in Myanmar?
14. What is the currency of Myanmar?
15. What is the largest city in Myanmar?
16. Which country is the major import partner of Myanmar?
17. Which country is the major export partner of Myanmar?
18. Which precious stone accounts for ninety percent coming from Myanmar?
19. Which country provides the most tourists to Myanmar?
20. What is the most popular sport in Myanmar?
21. Which side of the road do drivers in Myanmar drive on?
22. Which group of people in Myanmar have faced human rights abuses over the years?

23. What letters appear at the end of a web address from Myanmar?
24. What is the main ingredient in many food dishes from Myanmar?
25. What is the national and traditional sport of Myanmar?

MYANMAR ANSWERS

1. Burma
2. Asia
3. Republic of the Union of Myanmar
4. Naypyidaw
5. Five-India, Bangladesh, Thailand, Laos, China
6. Yellow, green, red
7. 53 million (2017 census)
8. United Kingdom
9. Parliamentary constitutional republic
10. Aung San Suu Kyi
11. Burmese
12. President
13. Buddhism
14. Kyat
15. Yangon
16. China
17. China
18. Ruby
19. Thailand
20. Football
21. Right hand side
22. Rohingya
23. .mm
24. Fish
25. Chinlone (caneball)

NETHERLANDS

1. What are the differences between the terms Holland and the Netherlands?
2. What are the colours of the flag of the Netherlands?
3. What is the capital of the Netherlands?
4. What form of government does the Netherlands have?
5. What is the official language of the Netherlands?
6. Between 15 and 20 million, what is the population of the Netherlands?
7. From which country did the Netherlands declare its independence in 1581?
8. What is the currency of the Netherlands?
9. How many countries share a land border with the Netherlands?
10. Which city in the Netherlands has Europe's largest port?
11. Which country invaded the Netherlands in World War II?
12. Who is the Head of State in the Netherlands?
13. Who is considered the most famous Dutch painter of the 17th century?
14. Which Dutch duo from the 1990s are the most successful music artists to this day?
15. What is the most popular participant sport in the Netherlands?
16. Which side of the road do drivers from the Netherlands drive on?
17. What successful company was set up by the Netherlands in the 17th century?

18. What letters appear at the end of a web page from the Netherlands?
19. Which Dutch painter severed part of his left ear, due to his mental health illness?
20. How many times has the Netherlands won the Eurovision Song Contest?
21. Which country provides the most tourists to the Netherlands?
22. What is the largest city in the Netherlands?
23. Which driver was the first Dutchman to win a Formula One Grand Prix race?
24. What is the name of the region that comprises Belgium, the Netherlands and Luxembourg called?
25. Which city is the seat of Government in the Netherlands?

NETHERLANDS ANSWERS

1. Holland is a region and former province of the Netherlands
2. Red, white, blue
3. Amsterdam
4. Parliamentary Constitutional Monarchy
5. Dutch
6. 17 million (2019 estimate)
7. Spain
8. Euro
9. Two-Germany, Belgium
10. Rotterdam
11. Germany
12. The Monarch
13. Rembrandt
14. 2 Unlimited
15. Football
16. Right hand side
17. Dutch East India Company
18. .nl (.bq)
19. Vincent van Gogh
20. Five times
21. Germany
22. Amsterdam
23. Max Verstappen
24. The Low Countries
25. The Hague

NEW ZEALAND

---

1. How many stars are on the New Zealand flag?
2. What are the official languages of New Zealand?
3. What is the capital city of New Zealand?
4. Which European explorer was the first to sight New Zealand?
5. Between one and five million, what is the population of New Zealand?
6. Aotearoa is the Maori name for New Zealand. What is it translated to in English?
7. Which explorer mapped almost the entire New Zealand coastline?
8. What is the largest city in New Zealand?
9. What famous document was signed by the British and Maori chiefs in 1840?
10. On which side of the road do New Zealand drivers drive?
11. How many women have served as Prime Minister of New Zealand?
12. Which is greater in area-the North Island or the South Island of New Zealand?
13. What is considered the national sport of New Zealand?
14. Which New Zealander was the first to reach the summit of Mount Everest?
15. Which JRR Tolkien book was filmed as a trilogy in New Zealand?
16. What letters are at the end of website from New Zealand?
17. Which group of people first settled in New Zealand in the 13th century?

18. How many women have served as Governor-General of New Zealand?

19. What is the currency of New Zealand?

20. Which security treaty links New Zealand to Australia and the United States of America?

21. What is the nickname used for people from New Zealand?

22. Who was the New Zealand bowler that was the first to take 400 wickets in Test cricket?

23. What is the nickname for the New Zealand rugby union team?

24. What is the highest selling New Zealand pop song of all time?

25. What is the third largest island of New Zealand, located south of the South Island?

NEW ZEALAND ANSWERS

1. Four
2. English, Maori, NZ Sign Language
3. Wellington
4. Abel Tasman
5. 4(.9) million (2019 estimate)
6. Land of the long white cloud
7. Captain James Cook
8. Auckland
9. Treaty of Waitangi
10. Left hand side
11. Three (Jenny Shipley, Helen Clark, Jacinta Adearn)
12. South Island
13. Rugby union
14. Sir Edmund Hillary
15. The Lord of the Rings
16. .nz
17. Polynesians
18. Three (Dame Silvia Cartwright, Dame Sian Elias, Dame Patsy Reddy)
19. New Zealand dollar
20. ANZUS
21. Kiwi
22. Sir Richard Hadlee
23. The All-Blacks
24. How Bizarre (OMC)
25. Stewart Island

NIGERIA

1. What is the capital city of Nigeria?
2. What is the official name of Nigeria?
3. How many countries share a land border with Nigeria?
4. What colours are on the flag of Nigeria?
5. What is the official language of Nigeria?
6. Which country did Nigeria gain its independence from?
7. What form of government does Nigeria have?
8. Between 195 and 200 million, what is the population of Nigeria?
9. Which country is Nigeria's main export partner?
10. What is the currency of Nigeria?
11. What is the largest city in Nigeria?
12. Who is the Head of State in Nigeria?
13. Which country is Nigeria's main import partner?
14. Which side of the road do drivers in Nigeria drive on?
15. What are the two main religions of Nigeria?
16. What is the most popular sport in Nigeria?
17. Who is the Head of Government in Nigeria?
18. In which sport did Nigeria become the first African nation to qualify for at the Winter Olympics?
19. In which category did Wole Soyinka become the first Nobel Prize laureate from Nigeria?
20. In which sport has Nigeria won most of its Olympic medals, including two gold medals, at the Summer Olympic Games?
21. What is Nigeria's main export?
22. What letters appear at the end of a web address from Nigeria?

23. What is the major tourist destination in Nigeria?
24. How many times has Nigeria won the African Cup of Nations football title?
25. What board game was made an official sport in Nigeria in the 1990s?

NIGERIA ANSWERS

1. Abuja
2. Federal Republic of Nigeria
3. Four-Niger, Benin, Chad, Cameroon
4. Green, white
5. English
6. United Kingdom
7. Federal presidential republic
8. 200 million (2019 estimate)
9. India
10. Naira
11. Lagos
12. President
13. China
14. Right hand side
15. Islam, Christian
16. Football
17. President
18. Two-man bobsled team (Women's)
19. Literature
20. Athletics
21. Crude petroleum
22. .ng
23. Lagos
24. Three times
25. Scrabble

NORTH MACEDONIA

1. What is the official name of North Macedonia?
2. What is the capital city of North Macedonia?
3. How many countries share a land border with North Macedonia?
4. From which country did North Macedonia gain its independence in 1991?
5. Between one and five million, what is the population of North Macedonia?
6. What colours are on the flag of North Macedonia?
7. What are the two official languages of North Macedonia?
8. With which country has North Macedonia had a dispute with the name of Macedonia?
9. What form of government does North Macedonia have?
10. What is the currency of North Macedonia?
11. Which country is the major export partner of North Macedonia?
12. Which day in September is the national day Independence Day celebrated in North Macedonia?
13. Which country provides the most tourists to North Macedonia?
14. Who is the Head of State in North Macedonia?
15. What is the largest city in North Macedonia?
16. What is the main religion of North Macedonia?
17. What are the two most popular sports in North Macedonia?
18. Which side of the road do drivers in North Macedonia drive on?
19. Who is the Head of Government in North Macedonia?

20. In which sport has North Macedonia won its only Summer Olympic Medal-bronze in 2000?
21. What is the best result North Macedonia has had at the Eurovision Song Contest?
22. What letters appear at the end of a web address from North Macedonia?
23. What is the name of the agreement that ended the dispute over North Macedonia's name?
24. What town is the most popular tourist destination in North Macedonia?
25. Which country annexed North Macedonia after the Balkan Wars of 1912-13?

NORTH MACEDONIA ANSWERS

1. Republic of North Macedonia
2. Skopje
3. Five-Kosovo. Bulgaria, Albania, Greece, Serbia
4. Yugoslavia
5. Two million (2017 estimate)
6. Red, yellow
7. Macedonian, Albanian
8. Greece
9. Parliamentary republic
10. Macedonian denar
11. Germany
12. September 8th
13. Turkey
14. President
15. Skopje
16. Eastern (Macedonian) Orthodox Church
17. Football, handball
18. Right hand side
19. Prime Minister
20. Wrestling
21. 12th in 2006
22. .mk
23. Prespa Agreement
24. Ohrid
25. Serbia

NORWAY

1. What is the capital city of Norway?
2. What is the official name for Norway?
3. What are the colours on the flag of Norway?
4. How many countries share a border with Norway?
5. Between five and ten million, what is the population of Norway?
6. What is the form of government in Norway?
7. What are the two main official languages of Norway?
8. Which country invaded Norway during the Second World War?
9. Because of long bursts of sunlight in summer, what is Norway often referred to as?
10. Who is the Head of State in Norway?
11. What are the biggest exports of Norway?
12. What is the currency of Norway?
13. On which side of the road do Norwegian drivers drive?
14. What letters appear at the end of a web address from Norway?
15. What is the state church of Norway?
16. How many Norwegian films have won the Academy Award for Best Foreign Language Film?
17. What is the most popular sport in Norway?
18. Which country is Norway's major export partner?
19. How many times has Norway won the Eurovision Song Contest?
20. Where does Norway rank in terms of medals won at the Winter Olympics?

21. What was Norway's status during the First World War?
22. Which Norwegian composer is considered one of the most influential romantic composers of all time?
23. What is the biggest indoor sport in Norway?
24. Which Norwegian painted the world famous painting "The Scream"?
25. What is the largest immigrant group in Norway?

NORWAY ANSWERS

1. Oslo
2. Kingdom of Norway
3. Red, white, blue
4. Four-Sweden, Denmark, Finland, Russia
5. Five(.3) million (2019 estimate)
6. Parliamentary Constitutional Monarchy
7. Norwegian, Sami
8. Germany
9. Land of the Midnight Sun
10. The Monarch
11. Petroleum and petroleum products
12. Norwegian krone
13. Right hand side
14. .no
15. Church of Norway
16. None
17. Football
18. United Kingdom
19. Three times-1985, 1995, 2009
20. First
21. Neutral
22. Edvard Grieg
23. Ice hockey
24. Edvard Munch
25. Polish (Poland)

PAKISTAN

1. What are the colours on the flag of Pakistan?
2. Which former Test cricketer became Prime Minister of Pakistan in 2018?
3. What is the official name of Pakistan?
4. What is the capital of Pakistan?
5. What are the two official languages of Pakistan?
6. How many countries share a border with Pakistan?
7. Who became Pakistan's first female Prime Minister in 1988?
8. Between 210 and 215 million, what is the population of Pakistan?
9. What side of the road do drivers in Pakistan drive on?
10. What is the currency of Pakistan?
11. Who is the Head of State in Pakistan?
12. Which Middle East country does Pakistan not have diplomatic relations with?
13. What are the letters at the end of a web address from Pakistan?
14. What is the most popular sport in Pakistan?
15. What is the state religion of Pakistan?
16. How many times has Pakistan won the Hockey World Cup?
17. What is the largest city in Pakistan?
18. Which country provides the most tourists to Pakistan?
19. What is the national language of Pakistan?
20. Which country is the major export partner of Pakistan?
21. Who is the Head of Government in Pakistan?
22. What is the national sport of Pakistan?

23. Who did Pakistan defeat to win the ICC Champions Trophy in 2017?
24. What is the main ethnic group in Pakistan?
25. Which area north of India and Pakistan is a major territorial conflict between the two nations?

PAKISTAN ANSWERS

1. Green and white
2. Imran Khan
3. Islamic Republic of Pakistan
4. Islamabad
5. English, Urdu
6. Three-India, Afghanistan, China
7. Benazir Bhutto
8. 212 million (2017 census)
9. Left hand side
10. Pakistani rupee
11. President
12. Israel
13. .pk
14. Cricket
15. Sunni Islam
16. Four times
17. Karachi
18. United Kingdom
19. Urdu
20. United States of America
21. Prime Minister
22. Field hockey
23. India
24. Punjabi
25. Kashmir

PANAMA

1. What are the colours on the flag of Panama?
2. What is the capital city of Panama?
3. What is the official name of Panama?
4. How many countries share a land border with Panama?
5. Between one and five million, what is the population of Panama?
6. From which country did Panama gain its independence in 1821?
7. What form of government does Panama have?
8. What is the official language of Panama?
9. In which year was the Panama Canal opened?
10. What are the two official currencies of Panama?
11. From which South American country did Panama secede in 1903?
12. What is the largest city in Panama?
13. Who is the Head of State in Panama?
14. Which country is the major export partner of Panama?
15. Which two oceans does the Panama Canal connect?
16. Which military leader was de facto ruler of Panama from 1983 to 1989?
17. Who is the Head of Government in Panama?
18. Which country provides the most tourists to Panama?
19. What is the national sport of Panama?
20. Which side of the road do drivers in Panama drive on?
21. What is the dominant religious denomination in Panama?
22. How many gold medals has Panama won at the Summer Olympic Games?

23. What letters appear at the end of a web address from Panama?
24. How long is the Panama Canal (in km or miles)?
25. What day in November is Panama's Independence Day Celebrated?

PANAMA ANSWERS

1. Red, white, blue
2. Panama City
3. Republic of Panama
4. Two-Costa Rica, Colombia
5. Four million (2016 estimate)
6. Spain
7. Presidential constitutional republic
8. Spanish
9. 1914
10. Balboa, US Dollar
11. Colombia
12. Panama City
13. President
14. United States of America
15. Atlantic, Pacific
16. Manuel Noriega
17. President
18. United States of America
19. Baseball
20. Right hand side
21. Roman Catholic
22. One-athletics
23. .pa
24. 82km (51miles)
25. November 28th

PAPUA NEW GUINEA

1. What is the official name of Papua New Guinea?
2. In which ocean is Papua New Guinea?
3. What is the capital city of Papua New Guinea?
4. What colours are on the flag of Papua New Guinea?
5. From which country did Papua New Guinea gain its independence in 1975?
6. What form of government does Papua New Guinea have?
7. What are the four official languages of Papua New Guinea?
8. Between five and ten million, what is the population of Papua New Guinea?
9. Who is the Head of State in Papua New Guinea?
10. Which country rules the western half of Papua New Guinea?
11. Which country is the major export partner of Papua New Guinea?
12. What is the largest city in Papua New Guinea?
13. What is the currency of Papua New Guinea?
14. What are the two main export commodities of Papua New Guinea?
15. Who is the Head of Government in Papua New Guinea?
16. What is the dominant religious denomination in Papua New Guinea?
17. What is the most popular sport in Papua New Guinea?
18. Which side of the road do drivers in Papua New Guinea drive on?
19. Which country is the major import partner of Papua New Guinea?

20. Which Papua New Guinea born Australian Rules football player played for the Brisbane Lions (3 Premierships), Essendon and Collingwood?

21. Which two countries controlled Papua New Guinea until 1919?

22. What letters appear at the end of a web address from Papua New Guinea?

23. How many medals has Papua New Guinea won at the Summer Olympic Games?

24. What symbol appears on both the flags of Papua New Guinea and Australia?

25. The New Guinea Campaign during World War Two was a conflict between soldiers of which three countries?

PAPUA NEW GUINEA ANSWERS

1. Independent State of Papua New Guinea
2. Pacific Ocean
3. Port Moresby
4. Red and black
5. Australia
6. Parliamentary constitutional monarchy
7. English, Hiri Motu, PNG sign language, Tok Pisin
8. Eight million (2016 census preliminary estimate)
9. British Monarch
10. Indonesia
11. Australia
12. Port Moresby
13. Papua New Guinean kina
14. Fuels and mining
15. Prime Minister
16. Roman Catholic
17. Rugby league
18. Left hand side
19. Australia
20. Mal Michael
21. Germany, United Kingdom
22. .pg
23. None
24. Southern Cross
25. Australia, United States, Japan

PARAGUAY

1. In which continent is Paraguay?
2. What is the official name of Paraguay?
3. What is the capital city of Paraguay?
4. What are the colours on the flag of Paraguay?
5. How many countries share a land border with Paraguay?
6. What form of government does Paraguay have?
7. Between five and ten million, what is the population of Paraguay?
8. What are the two official languages of Paraguay?
9. From which country did Paraguay declare its independence in 1811?
10. What is unusual about the flag of Paraguay?
11. Who is the Head of State in Paraguay?
12. What is the dominant religious denomination in Paraguay?
13. What is the currency of Paraguay?
14. What is the largest city in Paraguay?
15. Which country is Paraguay's major export partner?
16. Who is the Head of Government in Paraguay?
17. What is used to produce 99% of Paraguay's electricity?
18. What is Paraguay largest export commodity?
19. What is the most popular sport in Paraguay?
20. Which side of the road do drivers in Paraguay drive on?
21. In which sport has Paraguay won its only Summer Olympic Games medal-silver-in 2004?
22. Which country is Paraguay's major import partner?
23. What letters appear at the end of a web address from Paraguay?

24. What is the best place finish Paraguay has had at the FIFA World Cup of Football?
25. Which country provides the most tourists to Paraguay?

PARAGUAY ANSWERS

1. South America
2. Republic of Paraguay
3. Asuncion
4. Red, white, blue
5. Three-Argentina, Brazil, Bolivia
6. Dominant party presidential republic
7. Seven million (2019 estimate)
8. Spanish, Guarani
9. Spain
10. Differs on each side-obverse has the coat of arms and the reverse side has the seal of the treasury
11. President
12. Roman Catholic
13. Guarani
14. Asuncion
15. Brazil
16. President
17. Hydroelectric
18. Soya beans
19. Football
20. Right hand side
21. Football
22. Brazil
23. .py
24. 8th-2010
25. Argentina

PERU

1. What is the official name for Peru?
2. What is the capital city of Peru?
3. What colours are on the flag of Peru?
4. How many countries share a land border with Peru?
5. Which mountain range runs along Peru?
6. What is the official language of Peru?
7. Between 30 and 35 million, what is the population of Peru?
8. What form of government does Peru have?
9. From which country did Peru gain its independence in 1824?
10. What is the currency of Peru?
11. Who is the Head of State and Head of Government in Peru?
12. Which country is the major export partner of Peru?
13. Which lake in Peru is also the largest in South America?
14. What is the dominant religious denomination in Peru?
15. Which side of the road do drivers in Peru drive on?
16. What is the most popular sport in Peru?
17. How many gold medals has Peru won at the Summer Olympic Games?
18. Which country provides the most tourists to Peru?
19. How many times has Peru won the Copa America trophy in football?
20. What is the most visited tourist attraction in Peru?
21. What letters appear at the end of a web address from Peru?

22. Who was President of Peru from 1990 to 2000, and was later jailed for embezzlement?
23. Which empire in Peru was suppressed by the Spanish?
24. How many films from Peru have been nominated for Best Foreign Language Film at the Academy Awards?
25. Which major rainforest is partly in Peru?

PERU ANSWERS

1. Republic of Peru
2. Lima
3. Red, white
4. Five-Brazil, Chile, Ecuador, Colombia, Bolivia
5. Andes Mountains
6. Spanish
7. 32 million (2019 estimate)
8. Presidential republic
9. Spain
10. Sol
11. President
12. China
13. Lake Titicaca
14. Roman Catholic
15. Right hand side
16. Football
17. One
18. Chile
19. Twice
20. Machu Picchu
21. .pe
22. Alberto Fujimori
23. Inca Empire
24. One
25. Amazon rainforest

PHILIPPINES

1. What is the capital city of the Philippines?
2. What are the colours on the flag of the Philippines?
3. What is the official name of the Philippines?
4. The Philippines is bounded by how many seas?
5. What are the two official languages of the Philippines?
6. What form of government does the Philippines have?
7. From which country did the Philippines declare its independence in 1898?
8. What is the currency of the Philippines?
9. In what year of the 21st century did the population of the Philippines reach 100 million?
10. Who is the Head of State and Head of the Government in the Philippines?
11. What is the dominant religious denomination of the Philippines?
12. What side of the road do Philippine drivers drive on?
13. Who was President of the Philippines from 1965 to 1986?
14. What is the most popular sport in the Philippines?
15. What is the largest city in the Philippines?
16. Which country is the major export partner of the Philippines?
17. Who has been the most successful Philippine boxer in the world?
18. Who became the first female President of the Philippines in 1986?
19. What letters are at the end of a web address from the Philippines?
20. Which country provides the most tourists to the Philippines?

21. Who are the Philippines named after?
22. What type of natural disaster affects the Philippines annually?
23. What is the national sport of the Philippines?
24. What is the largest and most populous island of the Philippines?
25. Which country invaded the Philippines during World War Two?

PHILIPPINES ANSWERS

1. Manila
2. Red, white, blue, yellow
3. Republic of Philippines
4. Three-South China Sea, Philippine Sea, Celebes Sea
5. Filipino, English
6. Unitary Presidential Constitutional Republic
7. Spain
8. Peso
9. 2014
10. President
11. Roman Catholic
12. Right hand side
13. Ferdinand Marcos
14. Basketball
15. Quezon City
16. United States of America
17. Many Pacquiao
18. Corazon Aquino
19. .ph
20. South Korea
21. King Philip II of Spain
22. Cyclones (Typhoons)
23. Arnis (Eskrima or Kali) martial arts
24. Luzon
25. Japan

POLAND

1. What is the capital city of Poland?
2. What are the colours on the flag of Poland?
3. What is the official name of Poland?
4. Which countries invaded Poland in 1939?
5. How many countries share a land border with Poland?
6. What is the official language of Poland?
7. Between 35 and 40 million, what is the population of Poland?
8. What form of government does Poland have?
9. Which workers movement was established in Poland in 1980?
10. What is the currency of Poland?
11. Who is the Head of State in Poland?
12. What is the most visited city by tourists in Poland?
13. How many times has Poland won the Eurovision Song Contest?
14. What is the largest city in Poland?
15. What are the two most popular sports in Poland?
16. Who is regarded as Poland's best known classical musician?
17. Which side of the road do drivers in Poland drive on?
18. Which infamous concentration camp is located in Poland?
19. What is the dominant religion of Poland?
20. Which country provides the most tourists to Poland?
21. What letters appear at the end of a web address from Poland?

22. How many times has Poland won the Academy Award for Best Foreign Language Film?
23. Who is the only Pole to reign as Pope of the Roman Catholic Church?
24. Who became the first Polish driver to win a Formula One Grand Prix race?
25. Polish beautician Maksymilian Faktorowicz created which famous cosmetics company?

POLAND ANSWERS

1. Warsaw
2. Red, white
3. Republic of Poland
4. Germany, Soviet Union
5. Six-Germany, Czech Republic, Slovakia, Ukraine, Belarus, Lithuania (Kaliningrad)
6. Polish
7. 38 million (2017 estimate)
8. Semi-presidential republic
9. Solidarity
10. Polish zloty
11. President
12. Krakow
13. None
14. Warsaw
15. Volleyball, football
16. Fryderyk Chopin
17. Right hand side
18. Auschwitz-Birkenau
19. Roman Catholic
20. Germany
21. .pl
22. Once
23. Pope John Paul II
24. Robert Kubica
25. Max Factor

PORTUGAL

1. What are the colours on the flag of Portugal?
2. What is the official name for Portugal?
3. What is the capital city of Portugal?
4. Which country shares a border with Portugal?
5. What is the currency of Portugal?
6. Between 10 and 15 million, what is the population of Portugal?
7. On which side of the road do Portuguese drivers drive?
8. What are the two official languages of Portugal?
9. Which ocean lies to the west of Portugal?
10. Who is the Head of State in Portugal?
11. Where does Portugal rank as a wine exporting country?
12. What is the main religious denomination in Portugal?
13. How many times has Portugal won the Eurovision Song Contest?
14. What is the most popular sport in Portugal?
15. What letters are at the end of a web address from Portugal?
16. Which country is the major export partner of Portugal?
17. What is the largest city in Portugal?
18. Which football manager has been the most successful to come from Portugal?
19. Who is the Head of Government in Portugal?
20. On which peninsula does Portugal lie?
21. With which country did Portugal make an alliance with in 1373, which is still standing?
22. Which footballer is a major symbol of Portuguese football history, and considered as one of the greatest of all time?

23. On which side did Portugal fight during the Second World War?

24. Portugal was the first country in the world to abolish which prison sentence?

25. Which former Portuguese Prime Minister became Secretary-General of the United Nations in 2017?

PORTUGAL ANSWERS

1. Red and green
2. Portuguese Republic
3. Lisbon
4. Spain
5. Euro
6. 10(.2) million (2018 estimate)
7. Right hand side
8. Portuguese, Mirandese
9. Atlantic Ocean
10. President
11. Fifth in the world
12. Roman Catholic
13. Once-2017
14. Football
15. .pt
16. Spain
17. Lisbon
18. Jose Mourinho
19. Prime Minister
20. Iberian Peninsula
21. England
22. Eusebio
23. Neutral
24. Life imprisonment
25. Antonio Guterres

QATAR

1. What is the official name of Qatar?
2. What is the capital city of Qatar?
3. What colours are on the flag of Qatar?
4. How many countries share a land border with Qatar?
5. What is the official language of Qatar?
6. From which country did Qatar gain its independence in 1971?
7. What is the official religion of Qatar?
8. What form of government does Qatar have?
9. Between one and five million, what is the population of Qatar?
10. Which day in December is the national holiday, Qatar National Day?
11. Who is the Head of State in Qatar?
12. In which continent is Qatar located?
13. What is the main export commodity of Qatar?
14. What is the name of the main television and news network located in Qatar?
15. What is the most popular sport in Qatar?
16. Which country is the major export partner of Qatar?
17. Which side of the road do drivers in Qatar drive on?
18. Which sporting title did Qatar win in 2019, defeating Japan in the final?
19. Who is the Head of Government in Qatar?
20. What is the largest city in Qatar?
21. In which sport has Qatar obtained the majority of its medals at the Summer Olympic Games?

22. What letters appear at the end of a web address from Qatar?
23. What major sporting event will Qatar host in 2022?
24. Which country is the major import partner of Qatar?
25. Which airline is the state owned flag carrier of Qatar?

QATAR ANSWERS

1. State of Qatar
2. Doha
3. Maroon, white
4. One-Saudi Arabia
5. Arabic
6. United Kingdom
7. Islam
8. Constitutional monarchy
9. Two (.6) million (2017 estimate)
10. December 18th
11. Emir
12. Asia
13. Oil, natural gas
14. Al Jazeera
15. Football
16. Japan
17. Right hand side
18. Asian Cup of Football
19. Prime Minister
20. Doha
21. Athletics
22. .qa
23. FIFA World Cup of Football
24. United States of America
25. Qatar Airways

ROMANIA

1. What are the colours on the Romanian flag?
2. What is the capital of Romania?
3. How many countries share a border with Romania?
4. Which major European river flows through Romania?
5. Which Communist dictator ruled Romania from 1965 to 1989?
6. Between 15 and 20 million, what is the population of Romania?
7. What is the official language of Romania?
8. From which empire did Romania gain its independence in 1878?
9. Who was the last king of Romania before his abdication in 1947?
10. What is the currency of Romania?
11. How many women have been Prime Minister of Romania?
12. What is the largest city in Romania?
13. From which European country does Romania attract the most tourists?
14. Even though there is no state religion in Romania, with which religion do 81% of Romanians identify with?
15. Where does Romania rank as being a plum producer in the world?
16. The national holiday of Romania is Great Union Day. On what day in December is it celebrated?
17. What is the most popular sport in Romania?
18. Which Romanian tennis player won the women's singles title at Wimbledon in 2019?

19. Bran's Castle, also known as Dracula's Castle, is in which region of Romania?
20. Which mountain range runs through the centre of Romania?
21. On which side of the road do Romanian drivers drive?
22. Which Romanian gymnast was the first to receive a perfect score of 10 in an event at the 1976 Olympic Games?
23. Which football team was the first Romanian team to win the European Champions Cup (now Champions League) in 1986?
24. What letters are at the end of a web address from Romania?
25. How many times has Romania won the Eurovision Song Contest?

ROMANIA ANSWERS

1. Red, yellow, blue
2. Bucharest
3. Five-Bulgaria, Ukraine, Serbia, Hungary, Moldova
4. Danube River
5. Nicolae Ceausescu
6. 19 million (2019 estimate)
7. Romanian
8. Ottoman Empire
9. Michael I
10. Romanian Leu
11. One-Viorica Dancila elected in 2018
12. Bucharest
13. Moldova (2016)
14. Eastern Orthodox Church
15. Second
16. December 1st
17. Football-soccer
18. Simona Halep
19. Transylvania
20. Carpathian Mountains
21. Right had side
22. Nadia Comaneci
23. Steaua Bucuresti
24. .ro
25. None

RUSSIA

1. What is the official name of Russia?
2. Prior to 1991, what was Russia called?
3. What is the capital city of Russia?
4. What are the colours on the flag of Russia?
5. How many countries share a border with Russia?
6. What is the official language of Russia?
7. Who was the last Tsar of the Russian Empire?
8. What is the currency of Russia?
9. What side of the road do Russian drivers drive on?
10. Who is the Head of State in Russia?
11. In area, where does Russia rank in the world?
12. Who was the last Soviet leader in Russia?
13. Who was the first Russian in outer space?
14. How many Russians are Nobel Prize Laureates?
15. Between 145 and 150 million, what is the population of Russia?
16. What is the largest city in Russia?
17. What is the dominant religion of Russia?
18. How many times have the Olympic Games (Summer and Winter) been held in Russia?
19. Which two 19th century Russian writers have been described as the greatest novelists of all time?
20. How many times has Russia won the Eurovision Song Contest?
21. Which country provides the most tourists to Russia?
22. Russia Day, the National holiday of Russia, is held in which day in June?

23. What letters appear at the end of a web address from Russia?

24. Who became the first directly elected President of Russia in 1991?

25. In what year was the Russian Revolution that saw the end of the monarchy?

RUSSIA ANSWERS

1. Russian Federation
2. USSR (Union of Soviet Socialist Republics)
3. Moscow
4. Red, white, blue
5. Fourteen
6. Russian
7. Nicholas II
8. Russian ruble
9. Right hand side
10. President
11. Largest country in the world
12. Mikhail Gorbachev
13. Yuri Gagarin
14. 25
15. 147 million (2019 estimate)
16. Moscow
17. Russian Orthodox
18. Twice-1980, 2014
19. Leo Tolstoy, Fyodor Dostoevsky
20. Once-2008
21. Germany
22. June 12
23. .ru (.su)
24. Boris Yeltsin
25. 1917

RWANDA

1. What is the official name of Rwanda?
2. What colours are on the flag of Rwanda?
3. How many countries share a land border with Rwanda?
4. What is the capital city of Rwanda?
5. What form of government does Rwanda have?
6. Between 10 and 15 million, what is the population of Rwanda?
7. What are the four official languages of Rwanda?
8. From which country did Rwanda gain its independence in 1962?
9. Which two cash crops are the major exports of Rwanda?
10. In which year of the 1990s was the genocide which saw nearly a million people killed?
11. Who is the Head of State in Rwanda?
12. What is the dominant religious denomination in Rwanda?
13. What is the currency of Rwanda?
14. Which country is Rwanda's major export partner?
15. What is the most popular sport in Rwanda?
16. Which day in April is Genocide Memorial Day in Rwanda?
17. What is the most popular music genre in Rwanda?
18. Which side of the road do drivers in Rwanda drive on?
19. What is banned in Rwanda, and tourists are told not to bring them in?
20. At which form of the Olympics has Rwanda gained its only medal?
21. What is the largest city in Rwanda?

22. Rwanda and Uganda are the only two countries where people can safely visit which type of primate?
23. What letters appear at the end of a web address from Rwanda?
24. Which country is Rwanda's major import trading partner?
25. How many times has Rwanda appeared at the African Cup of Nations football competition?

RWANDA ANSWERS

1. Republic of Rwanda
2. Blue, yellow, green
3. Four-Uganda, Tanzania, Democratic Republic of Congo, Burundi
4. Kigali
5. Dominant party presidential republic
6. 11 million (2015 estimate)
7. English, French, Swahili, Kinyarwanda
8. Belgium
9. Coffee, tea
10. 1994
11. President
12. Roman Catholic
13. Rwandan franc
14. Kenya
15. Football
16. April 7th
17. Hip hop
18. Right hand side
19. Plastic bags
20. Paralympics
21. Kigali
22. Mountain gorilla
23. .rw
24. Kenya
25. Once-2004

SAUDI ARABIA

1. What is the official name of Saudi Arabia?
2. What is the capital of Saudi Arabia?
3. What colours are on the flag of Saudi Arabia?
4. How many countries share a land border with Saudi Arabia?
5. What form of government does Saudi Arabia have?
6. What is the official language of Saudi Arabia?
7. Between 30 and 35 million, what is the population of Saudi Arabia?
8. In what year of the 1930s was Saudi Arabia founded?
9. What is the main export of Saudi Arabia?
10. What is the main religion of Saudi Arabia?
11. What is the largest city in Saudi Arabia?
12. On what day in November is the national holiday Saudi National Day?
13. What is the currency of Saudi Arabia?
14. Which country provides the most tourists to Saudi Arabia?
15. What is the national sport of Saudi Arabia?
16. Which side of the road do drivers in Saudi Arabia drive on?
17. In what year were Saudi women first allowed to drive cars?
18. How many times has Saudi Arabia won the AFC Asian Cup of football?
19. What percentage of drinking water in Saudi Arabia comes from desalination?
20. Which country is the major export partner of Saudi Arabia?
21. How many gold medals has Saudi Arabia won at the Summer Olympic Games?

22. What letters appear at the end of a web address from Saudi Arabia?
23. What is the name of the ruling royal family in Saudi Arabia?
24. Which journalist was murdered in the Saudi Arabian consulate in Istanbul in October 2018?
25. Who is the Head of State and Head of Government in Saudi Arabia?

SAUDI ARABIA ANSWERS

1. Kingdom of Saudi Arabia
2. Riyadh
3. Green, white
4. Eight-Qatar, Yemen, Bahrain, Jordan, Iraq, Kuwait, Oman, UAE
5. Islamic totalitarian absolute monarchy
6. Arabic
7. 33 million (2018 estimate)
8. 1932
9. Petroleum
10. Islam
11. Riyadh
12. September 23rd
13. Saudi riyal
14. Bangladesh
15. Football
16. Right hand side
17. 2018
18. Three times
19. 50%
20. China
21. None
22. .sa
23. House of Saud
24. Jamal Khashoggi
25. King

SCOTLAND

1. What is the capital city of Scotland?
2. What are the colours on the flag of Scotland?
3. How many countries share a land border with Scotland?
4. What is the official name of Scotland?
5. Which country is Scotland a part of?
6. What is the official language of Scotland?
7. What form of government does Scotland have?
8. What is the currency of Scotland?
9. Between five and ten million, what is the population of Scotland?
10. What is the national Church of Scotland?
11. Who is the Head of State in Scotland?
12. In which year of the 21st century was there a referendum on Scottish independence?
13. Which side of the road do drivers in Scotland drive on?
14. What is the largest city in Scotland?
15. Who is the Head of Government in Scotland?
16. Which flower is the national emblem of Scotland?
17. Which country provides the most tourists to Scotland?
18. What is Scotland's most recognisable musical instrument?
19. Who is regarded as the national poet of Scotland?
20. What is Scotland's national day, held on November 30th?
21. Which have been the two most successful clubs in Scottish football?
22. What is the largest tourist destination of Scotland?
23. Scotland is promoted as the home of which sport?

24. How many times has Scotland hosted the Commonwealth Games?
25. Which Scottish inventor demonstrated the first working television system in 1926?

SCOTLAND ANSWERS

1. Edinburgh
2. Blue, white
3. One-England
4. Scotland
5. United Kingdom
6. English
7. Devolved parliamentary legislature within a constitutional monarchy
8. Pound sterling
9. Five(.4) million (2017 estimate)
10. Church of Scotland
11. British Monarch
12. 2014
13. Left hand side
14. Glasgow
15. First Minister
16. Thistle
17. United States
18. Bagpipes
19. Robert Burns
20. St Andrew's Day
21. Rangers, Celtic
22. Edinburgh
23. Golf
24. Three times-1970, 1986, 2014
25. John Logie Baird

SENEGAL

1. What is the capital city of Senegal?
2. What colours are on the flag of Senegal?
3. What is the official name of Senegal?
4. How many countries share a land border with Senegal?
5. What is the official language of Senegal?
6. What form of government does Senegal have?
7. Between 10 and 15 million, what is the population of Senegal?
8. From which country did Senegal gain its independence in 1960?
9. Which country is the major export partner of Senegal?
10. Which city in Senegal was the traditional car rally finishing point?
11. What is the currency of Senegal?
12. Who is the Head of State in Senegal?
13. Which products are Senegal's main exports in trade?
14. What is the predominant religion in Senegal?
15. Which two sports are the most popular in Senegal?
16. What is the largest city in Senegal?
17. Which side of the road do drivers in Senegal drive on?
18. Who is the Head of Government in Senegal?
19. Which country is Senegal's main export partner?
20. How many medals has Senegal won at the Summer Olympic Games?
21. Which country from Europe provides the most tourists in Senegal?
22. In which continent is Senegal?

23. Which Senegalese footballer plays in the Premier League team of Liverpool (as of 2019)
24. What letters appear at the end of a web address from Senegal?
25. What is the primary crop of Senegal?

SENEGAL ANSWERS

1. Dakar
2. Green, yellow, red
3. Republic of Senegal
4. Five-Mauritania, The Gambia, Mali, Guinea, Guinea-Bissau
5. French
6. Semi-presidential republic
7. 14 million (2016 census)
8. France
9. Mali
10. Dakar
11. West African CFA franc
12. President
13. Fish products
14. Islam
15. Wrestling, football
16. Dakar
17. Right hand side
18. Prime Minister
19. India
20. One-silver 1988(athletics)
21. France
22. Africa
23. Sadio Mane
24. .sn
25. Peanuts

SERBIA

1. What is the capital city of Serbia?
2. What colours are on the flag of Serbia?
3. What is the official name of Serbia?
4. How many countries share a land border with Serbia?
5. Between five and ten million, what is the population of Serbia?
6. What is the official language of Serbia?
7. What form of government does Serbia have?
8. In what year of the 2000s was Serbia declared an independent republic?
9. What is the currency of Serbia?
10. Who is the Head of State in Serbia?
11. Serbia was part of which larger country after World War One?
12. Which large European river passes through Serbia?
13. What is the largest city in Serbia?
14. Who is the Head of Government in Serbia?
15. What is the dominant church in Serbia?
16. Which country provides the most tourists to Serbia?
17. What is the most popular sport in Serbia?
18. Which side of the road do drivers in Serbia drive on?
19. Who has been the most successful Serbian tennis player?
20. What is considered the national drink of Serbia?
21. How many times has Serbia won the Eurovision Song Contest?
22. In which sport has Serbia been a world champion twice?

23. What are the letters at the end of a web address from Serbia?

24. Which Serbian leader was indicted of war crimes in 1999?

25. Which country is the major export partner of Serbia?

SERBIA ANSWERS

1. Belgrade
2. Red, white, blue
3. Republic of Serbia
4. Seven (Eight)-Bulgaria, Romania, Montenegro, Bosnia & Herzegovina, Hungary, Croatia, Macedonia (Albania-via Kosovo)
5. Seven million (2019 estimate)
6. Serbian
7. Parliamentary constitutional republic
8. 2006
9. Serbian dinar
10. President
11. Yugoslavia
12. Danube
13. Belgrade
14. Prime Minister
15. Serbian Orthodox Church
16. Bosnia & Herzegovina
17. Football
18. Right hand side
19. Novak Djokovic
20. Slivovitz
21. Once-2007
22. Men's basketball
23. .rs
24. Slobodan Milosevic
25. Italy

SINGAPORE

1. What is the capital city of Singapore?
2. What are the colours on the flag of Singapore?
3. What is the official name for Singapore?
4. Which country invaded Singapore during World War Two?
5. From which country did Singapore gain its independence in 1963?
6. How many official languages are there in Singapore?
7. Between five and ten million, what is the population of Singapore?
8. What is the currency of Singapore?
9. Who was the first Prime Minister and founding father of Singapore?
10. What form of government does Singapore have?
11. Which airport in Singapore has been rated the World's Best Airport from 2013-2018?
12. Which side of the road do Singapore drivers drive on?
13. Which country provides the most tourists to Singapore?
14. What is the largest ethnic group in Singapore?
15. What is the most widely practised religion in Singapore?
16. What is said to be Singapore's national pastime?
17. For which sport did Singapore win its first Olympic Gold Medal in 2016?
18. What letters appear at the end of a web address from Singapore?
19. Which country is the major export partner of Singapore?
20. Which airline from Singapore was voted World's Best Airline in 2018?

21. With which other country did Singapore merge with briefly in the 1960s?
22. Who is the Head of Government in Singapore?
23. What was significant about the first Formula Grand Prix held in Singapore in 2008?
24. How many Prime Ministers have there been of Singapore since self-government? (As of 2018)
25. What district is considered the centre of tourism in Singapore?

SINGAPORE ANSWERS

1. Singapore
2. Red, white
3. Republic of Singapore
4. Japan
5. United Kingdom
6. Four-English, Malay, Tamil, Mandarin
7. Five(.6) million (2018 estimate)
8. Singapore dollar
9. Lee Kuan Yew
10. Parliamentary republic
11. Changi Airport
12. Left hand side
13. China
14. Chinese
15. Buddhism
16. Dining
17. Swimming-butterfly
18. .sg
19. China
20. Singapore Airlines
21. Malaysia
22. Prime Minister
23. First one held at night
24. Three
25. Orchard Road

SLOVAKIA

1. What is the official name of Slovakia?
2. What is the capital of Slovakia?
3. How many countries share a land border with Slovakia?
4. What are the colours on the flag of Slovakia?
5. Between five and ten million, what is the population of Slovakia?
6. What is the official language of Slovakia?
7. What form of government does Slovakia have?
8. Which larger country was Slovakia a part of before 1993?
9. What is the currency of Slovakia?
10. A Slovak Republic was created in 1939 and sided with which country?
11. Who is the Head of State in Slovakia?
12. Which country is the major export partner of Slovakia?
13. What is the largest city in Slovakia?
14. What is Slovakia's biggest export?
15. Which country provides the most tourists to Slovakia?
16. What is the dominant religious denomination in Slovakia?
17. What is the most popular sport in Slovakia?
18. Which side of the road do drivers in Slovakia drive on?
19. Who are the Patron Saints of Slovakia?
20. In which sport has Slovakia won eight gold medals at the Summer Olympic Games?
21. What is the most popular tourist destination in Slovakia?
22. What is the best place finish Slovakia has had at the Eurovision Song Contest?

23. Who is the Head of Government in Bratislava?
24. What accounts for over half of electricity production in Slovakia?
25. What letters are at the end of a web address from Slovakia?

SLOVAKIA ANSWERS

1. Slovak Republic
2. Bratislava
3. Red, blue, white
4. Five-Poland, Austria, Ukraine, Czech Republic, Hungary
5. Five(.4) million (2018 estimate)
6. Slovak
7. Parliamentary republic
8. Czechoslovakia
9. Euro
10. Germany
11. President
12. Germany
13. Bratislava
14. Automobiles
15. Czech Republic
16. Roman Catholic
17. Football
18. Right hand side
19. Cyril and Methodius
20. Canoeing
21. Bratislava
22. 18th-1996
23. Prime Minister
24. Nuclear energy
25. .sk

SLOVENIA

1. What is the official name of Slovenia?
2. What is the capital city of Slovenia?
3. What colours are on the flag of Slovenia?
4. How many countries share a land border with Slovenia?
5. What is the official language of Slovenia?
6. From which country did Slovenia split to become an independent country in 1991?
7. Which three countries occupied and annexed Slovenia in 1941?
8. What form of government does Slovenia have?
9. What is the currency of Slovenia?
10. Between one and five million, what is the population of Slovenia?
11. Who is the Head of State in Slovenia?
12. What is the biggest export of Slovenia?
13. Which country provides the most tourists to Slovenia?
14. What is the largest city in Slovenia?
15. What is the dominant religious denomination in Slovenia?
16. In which sport has Slovenia won the most gold medals at the Summer Olympic Games?
17. Which side of the road do drivers in Slovenia drive on?
18. Who is the Head of Government in Slovenia?
19. What is the largest airline in Slovenia?
20. What letters appear at the end of a website from Slovenia?
21. What is the best placed finish that Slovenia has had at the Eurovision Song Contest?
22. Which country is the major export partner of Slovenia?

23. In which sport has Slovenia won its only Gold medals in the Winter Olympic Games?
24. Which sea is to the southwest of Slovenia?
25. What is the retirement age for men and women respectively in Slovenia?

SLOVENIA ANSWERS

1. Republic of Slovenia
2. Ljubljana
3. Red, white, blue
4. Four-Austria, Italy, Hungary, Croatia
5. Slovene
6. Yugoslavia
7. Germany, Italy, Hungary
8. Parliamentary constitutional republic
9. Euro
10. Two million (2018 estimate)
11. President
12. Automobiles
13. Italy
14. Ljubljana
15. Roman Catholic
16. Judo
17. Right hand side
18. Prime Minister
19. Adria Airways
20. .sl
21. Seventh (twice)
22. Germany
23. Alpine skiing
24. Adriatic Sea
25. 58 for men, 57 for women

SOUTH AFRICA

1. What is the currency of South Africa?
2. Which colours are on the flag of South Africa?
3. In what year did the Boer War, between the British and the Boer Republics conclude?
4. What are the three main sports played in South Africa?
5. Who was the last white President of South Africa?
6. Between 55 and 60 million, what is the population of South Africa?
7. In what year was Nelson Mandela elected the first black President of South Africa?
8. What is South Africa's largest city?
9. How many official languages are there in South Africa?
10. Which South African athlete became the first double amputee to compete in the 2012 Olympic Games in London?
11. What letters are used at the end of a South African internet address?
12. What side of the road do South African drivers drive on?
13. In what year of the 1960s did South Africa proclaim itself as the Republic of South Africa?
14. Which is the largest province in South Africa, in area and population?
15. What is the largest Christian denomination in South Africa?
16. Who is regarded as the greatest South African golfer of all time?
17. How many years did Nelson Mandela serve in prison before being released in 1990?

18. How many times has South Africa won the Rugby World Cup?
19. Which mountain overlooks Cape Town?
20. Who has been South Africa's longest serving cricket captain?
21. From which country does South Africa attract the most tourists?
22. Which political party was in government in South Africa from 1948 to 1994?
23. Which South African born cricketer was at the centre of a sporting controversy between England and South Africa in 19868?
24. What is the name of South Africa's first National Park?
25. What is unusual about South Africa's capital city?

SOUTH AFRICA ANSWERS

1. South African Rand
2. Red, green, blue, white, yellow, black
3. 1902
4. Rugby, cricket, football (soccer)
5. FW de Klerk
6. 57 million (2018 estimate)
7. 1994
8. Johannesburg
9. Eleven
10. Oscar Pistorius
11. .za
12. Left hand side
13. 1961
14. Eastern Cape
15. Protestant
16. Gary Player
17. 27 years
18. Twice-1995 and 2007
19. Table Mountain
20. Graeme Smith
21. Zimbabwe
22. National Party
23. Basil D'Oliveira
24. Kruger National Park
25. South Africa has no legally defined capital city-Cape Town is the legislative capital, Pretoria is the administrative capital and Bloemfontein is the judicial capital

SPAIN

1. What is the official name of Spain?
2. What is the currency used in Spain called?
3. Between 45 and 50 million, what is the population of Spain?
4. In what year did the Spanish Civil War begin in Spain?
5. What is the capital city of Spain?
6. What is the official language of Spain?
7. Who led the Nationalist forces during the Spanish Civil War?
8. What is the dominant religious denomination in Spain?
9. What two football clubs have been the most dominant in Spanish and European competitions?
10. Who has been the most successful male tennis player to come from Spain?
11. Where in Spain is the famous running of the bulls held?
12. What is the most well-known rice dish from Spain called?
13. Who became king of Spain after the restoration of democracy in Spain in 1978?
14. Which region of Spain held a referendum in 2017 on declaring independence from Spain?
15. Who is the current monarch in Spain (as of 2018)?
16. What was Spain ranked in the world in terms of tourism numbers in 2017?
17. What side of the road do Spanish drivers drive on?
18. What was the name of the fleet sent by Spain to invade England in 1588?
19. What was the Roman name for Spain?
20. In what year did Spain win the FIFA World Cup of football?

21. Which Spanish motorcycle rider has won the MotoGP World Championship four times (as of 2018)?

22. Which two Spanish tenors appeared with Luciano Pavarotti as part of The Three Tenors?

23. Which Spanish rider has won the Tour de France five times?

24. Which Spanish city hosted the 1992 Summer Olympic Games?

25. What is the largest city in Spain?

SPAIN ANSWERS

1. Kingdom of Spain
2. Euro
3. 46 million (2019 estimate)
4. 1936
5. Madrid
6. Spanish (Castilian)
7. General Francisco Franco
8. Roman Catholic
9. Barcelona, Real Madrid
10. Rafael Nadal
11. Pamplona
12. Paella
13. King Juan Carlos
14. Catalan
15. King Felipe VI
16. 2nd in the world
17. Right hand side
18. Spanish Armada
19. Hispania (Citerior and Ulterior)
20. 2010
21. Marc Marquez
22. Placido Domingo, Jose Carreras
23. Miguel Indurain
24. Barcelona
25. Madrid

SRI LANKA

1. What is the capital of Sri Lanka?
2. What is the official name of Sri Lanka?
3. What colours are on the flag of Sri Lanka?
4. By what name was Sri Lanka known as previously?
5. What are the two official languages of Sri Lanka?
6. From which country did Sri Lanka gain its independence?
7. Palk Strait separates Sri Lanka from which country?
8. What is the currency of Sri Lanka?
9. Between 20 and 25 million, what is the population of Sri Lanka?
10. What form of government does Sri Lanka have?
11. In which year of the 1970s did the name change to Sri Lanka occur?
12. Sri Lankan Sirimavo Bandaranaike became the first what in the world in 1960?
13. Who is the Head of State and Head of Government in Sri Lanka?
14. What is the dominant religion in Sri Lanka?
15. Which country is the major export partner of Sri Lanka?
16. What is the national sport of Sri Lanka?
17. Which side of the road do drivers in Sri Lanka drive on?
18. Which cash crop is Sri Lanka's biggest export?
19. What is the most popular sport in Sri Lanka?
20. Which country provides the biggest number of tourists to Sri Lanka?
21. What letters are at the end of a web address from Sri Lanka?

22. Which major sporting trophy did Sri Lanka win in 1996?
23. A 30 year civil war ended in 2009 when the Sri Lankan armed forces defeated which group?
24. Which Sri Lankan cricketer holds the record for most Test and one day wickets?
25. What natural disaster struck Sri Lanka in late 2004, killing over 35000 people?

SRI LANKA ANSWERS

1. Colombo (Sri Jayawardenepura Kotte-administrative capital)
2. Democratic Socialist Republic of Sri Lanka
3. Maroon, gold, green, saffron
4. Ceylon
5. Sinhala, Tamil
6. United Kingdom
7. India
8. Sri Lankan rupee
9. 21 million (2018 estimate)
10. Semi-presidential constitutional republic
11. 1972
12. First female Prime Minister
13. President
14. Buddhism
15. United States of America
16. Volleyball
17. Left hand side
18. Tea
19. Cricket
20. India
21. .lk
22. World Cup of cricket
23. Tamil separatists
24. Muttiah Muralitharan (Muralidaran)
25. Tsunami

SWEDEN

1. What are the colours on the flag of Sweden?
2. What is the official name of Sweden?
3. Between 10 and 15 million, what is the population of Sweden?
4. Who is the Head of State in Sweden?
5. What is the capital of Sweden?
6. What is the currency of Sweden?
7. What is the official language of Sweden?
8. Until 2000, what was the state religion of Sweden?
9. Who is considered the most successful music export of Sweden?
10. What are the two major spectator sports in Sweden?
11. How many times has Sweden hosted the Summer Olympic Games?
12. How many times has Sweden won the Eurovision Song Contest?
13. What is the largest city in Sweden?
14. Which Swedish chemist invented dynamite?
15. On which side of the road do Swedish drivers drive?
16. Which male Swedish tennis player won five consecutive Wimbledon titles?
17. Which Swedish company has been the world's largest furniture retailer since 2008?
18. How many times has the Swedish men's ice hockey team won the Gold medal at the Winter Olympics?
19. What day in June is celebrated as National Day of Sweden?

20. What every day invention for storing liquid foods, beverages and ice cream was invented by Swedish inventor Erik Wallenberg?

21. Who is considered Sweden's most successful women's golfer?

22. What letters are at the end of a web address from Sweden?

23. Which countries share a natural border with Sweden?

24. Who is the Head of Government in Sweden?

25. In terms of area, what ranking does Sweden have in Europe in relation to size?

SWEDEN ANSWERS

1. Blue and yellow
2. Kingdom of Sweden
3. Ten(.2) million (2019 census)
4. The Monarch (King Gustav XVI-as of 2018)
5. Stockholm
6. Swedish krona
7. Swedish
8. Lutheran Church of Sweden
9. ABBA
10. Football, ice hockey
11. Once (1912-Stockholm)
12. Six times
13. Stockholm
14. Alfred Nobel
15. Right hand side
16. Bjorn Borg
17. IKEA
18. Twice-1994, 2006
19. June 6th
20. Tetra Pak
21. Annika Sorenstam
22. .se
23. Norway, Finland
24. Prime Minister
25. Fifth largest in Europe

SWITZERLAND

1. What is the capital city of Switzerland?
2. What are the four official languages of Switzerland?
3. What is the currency of Switzerland?
4. What is the official name of Switzerland?
5. In what year of the 19th century did Switzerland gain independence and its right to neutrality?
6. Between five and ten million, what is the population of Switzerland?
7. What is Switzerland's main economic sector?
8. How many universities are there in Switzerland?
9. What is the largest city in Switzerland?
10. Which Swiss author wrote the classic children's story 'Heidi'?
11. In what year did Switzerland host the FIFA World Cup of football?
12. Who is the most successful Swiss tennis player in history?
13. In which Swiss city is the International Olympic Committee (IOC) based?
14. What is the most popular alcoholic drink in Switzerland?
15. Where do the Swiss rank in the world as consumers of chocolate?
16. What is the largest lake in Switzerland?
17. What letters appear at the end of a webpage that comes from Switzerland?
18. On what side of the road do Swiss drivers drive?
19. How many cantons (states) are there in Switzerland?
20. What are the colours on the flag of Switzerland?

21. In what year of the 21st century did Switzerland become a full member of the United Nations?
22. Which Swiss city is the birthplace of the Red Cross?
23. How many times has Switzerland hosted the Winter Olympic Games?
24. How many countries share a border with Switzerland?
25. How many times has Switzerland won the America's Cup of yachting?

SWITZERLAND ANSWERS

1. None-Bern is the de facto capital
2. German, French, Italian, Romansh
3. Swiss franc
4. Swiss Confederation
5. 1815
6. Eight million (2018 estimate)
7. Manufacturing
8. Twelve
9. Zurich
10. Johanna Spyri
11. 1954
12. Roger Federer
13. Lausanne
14. Wine
15. Number one in the world
16. Lake Geneva
17. .ch .swiss
18. Right hand side
19. Twenty six
20. Red and white
21. 2002
22. Geneva
23. Twice (1928, 1948)
24. Five (Germany, Italy, France, Austria, Liechtenstein)
25. Twice (2007, 2010)

SYRIA

1. What is the official name of Syria?
2. What are the colours on the flag of Syria?
3. How many countries share a land border with Syria?
4. What is the capital city of Syria?
5. What is the official language of Syria?
6. Between 15 and 20 million, what is the population of Syria?
7. From which country did Syria gain its independence?
8. What form of government does Syria have?
9. What is the dominant religion in Syria?
10. Who is the Head of State in Syria?
11. What is the largest city in Syria?
12. What is the currency of Syria?
13. Which empire ruled Syria for 400 years?
14. What has decimated export and tourist revenue for Syria since 2011?
15. What is the major export commodity of Syria?
16. What is the most popular sport in Syria?
17. Which country is Syria's major export partner?
18. Who is the Head of Government in Syria?
19. Which side of the road do drivers in Syria drive on?
20. How many medals in total has Syria won at Summer Olympic Games?
21. Approximately how many Syrians are displaced refugees out of Syria?
22. Which city in Syria is one of the oldest continuously inhabited cities in the world?

23. How many times has Syria qualified for the FIFA World Cup of football?
24. What letters appear at the end of a web address from Syria?
25. Which country is Syria's major import partner?

SYRIA ANSWERS

1. Syrian Arab Republic
2. Red, white, black green
3. Five-Iraq, Jordan, Lebanon, Israel, Turkey
4. Damascus
5. Arabic
6. 18 million (2019 estimate)
7. France
8. Dominant party semi-presidential republic
9. Islam
10. President
11. Damascus
12. Syrian pound
13. Ottoman Empire
14. Syrian Civil War
15. Oil
16. Football
17. Lebanon
18. Prime Minister
19. Right hand side
20. Three-one each of gold, silver, bronze
21. Five million
22. Aleppo
23. None
24. .sy
25. Russia

THAILAND

---

1. What is the capital city of Thailand?
2. What is the official name of Thailand?
3. What colours are on the flag of Thailand?
4. How many countries share a border with Thailand?
5. Between 65 and 70 million, what is the population of Thailand?
6. What was Thailand called previously?
7. What is the currency of Thailand?
8. What is the main religion of Thailand?
9. Who did Thailand declare war on in January 1942?
10. What form of government operates in Thailand?
11. What is the animal symbol of Thailand?
12. What is the largest industry in Thailand?
13. On which side of the road do Thailand's drivers drive?
14. What letters are at the end of a web address from Thailand?
15. What is the largest city in Thailand?
16. What is Thailand's signature sport?
17. What is the staple food in Thailand?
18. What is the official language of Thailand?
19. Which country provides the most tourists to Thailand?
20. Which sea lies to west of Thailand?
21. What powers 75% of Thailand's electricity generation?
22. What is the most popular sport in Thailand?
23. What form is used to count years in Thailand?
24. Thailand has won all its Olympic medals in which branches of men's and women's sports?
25. Who is the Head of State in Thailand?

THAILAND ANSWERS

1. Bangkok
2. Kingdom of Thailand
3. Red, white and blue
4. Four-Laos, Myanmar, Cambodia, Malaysia
5. 68 million (2016 estimate)
6. Siam
7. Baht
8. Buddhism
9. United States of America
10. Constitutional Monarchy
11. Elephant
12. Automotive industry
13. Left hand side
14. .th
15. Bangkok
16. Muay Thai-form of kickboxing
17. Rice
18. Thai
19. China
20. Andaman Sea
21. Natural gas
22. Football
23. Buddhist Era-543 years ahead of the Gregorian calendar
24. Men's boxing, women's weightlifting
25. The King

TONGA

1. What is the official name of Tonga?
2. What is the capital city of Tonga?
3. What colours are on the flag of Tonga?
4. How many countries share a land border with Tonga?
5. Between 100000 and 500000, what is the population of Tonga?
6. What form of government does Tonga have?
7. What are the two official languages of Tonga?
8. Tonga was a protected state under which country until 1970?
9. What is the state church of Tonga?
10. Who is the Head of State in Tonga?
11. What is the currency of Tonga?
12. Which country is the main export partner of Tonga?
13. What is the largest city in Tonga?
14. What is the national sport of Tonga?
15. Who is the Head of Government in Tonga?
16. In which sport has Tonga won its only Olympic medal at the Summer Olympic Games?
17. Which side of the road do drivers in Tonga drive on?
18. What colour is the cross on the flag of Tonga?
19. Which country is the major import partner of Tonga?
20. Tonga became known as the what islands after Captain Cook's visit in 1773?
21. Which animal is considered sacred in Tonga and cannot be harmed or hunted?

22. What fraction of Tonga's exports is from the agricultural sector?
23. What letters appear at the end of a web address from Tonga?
24. On which day of the week does all commerce and entertainment cease for the whole 24 hours?
25. What is considered the main health issue in Tonga?

TONGA ANSWERS

1. Kingdom of Tonga
2. Nuku'alofa
3. Red, white
4. None
5. 100000 (2016 census)
6. Parliamentary constitutional monarchy
7. English, Tongan
8. United Kingdom
9. Free Wesleyan Church of Tonga
10. Monarch
11. Pa'anga
12. South Korea
13. Nuku'alofa
14. Rugby union
15. Prime Minister
16. Boxing-1996-silver medal
17. Left hand side
18. Red
19. Fiji
20. Friendly Islands
21. Flying fox bats
22. Two thirds
23. .to
24. Sunday
25. Obesity

TRINIDAD AND TOBAGO

1. What is the official name of Trinidad and Tobago?
2. What is the capital city of Trinidad and Tobago?
3. How many countries share a land border with Trinidad and Tobago?
4. What colours are on the flag of Trinidad and Tobago?
5. From which country did Trinidad and Tobago gain its independence in 1962?
6. What form of government does Trinidad and Tobago have?
7. Between one and five million, what is the population of Trinidad and Tobago?
8. What is the currency of Trinidad and Tobago?
9. What is the main export of Trinidad and Tobago?
10. Who is the Head of State in Trinidad and Tobago?
11. Which airline is the flag carrier of Trinidad and Tobago?
12. What is the largest city in Trinidad and Tobago?
13. What is the official language of Trinidad and Tobago?
14. In what sea is Trinidad and Tobago located?
15. Which side of the road do drivers in Trinidad and Tobago drive on?
16. Which country is the major export partner of Trinidad and Tobago?
17. In which sport has Trinidad and Tobago won 15 of 19 medals at the Summer Olympic Games?
18. Which country provides the most tourists to Trinidad and Tobago?
19. Which record breaking cricketing batsman was born in Trinidad and Tobago?

20. Who is the Head of Government in Trinidad and Tobago?
21. Which musical instrument was invented in Trinidad and Tobago?
22. What is the national sport of Trinidad and Tobago?
23. What letters appear at the end of a web address from Trinidad and Tobago?
24. What is the dominant religious denomination in Trinidad and Tobago?
25. How many women from Trinidad and Tobago have been crowned Miss Universe?

TRINIDAD AND TOBAGO ANSWERS

1. Republic of Trinidad and Tobago
2. Port of Spain
3. None
4. Red, white, black
5. United Kingdom
6. Parliamentary constitutional republic
7. One(.3) million (2018 estimate)
8. Trinidad and Tobago dollar
9. Petroleum products
10. President
11. Caribbean Airlines
12. Chaguanas
13. English
14. Caribbean Sea
15. Left hand side
16. United States of America
17. Athletics
18. United States of America
19. Brian Lara
20. Prime Minister
21. Steelpan
22. Cricket
23. .tt
24. Roman Catholic
25. Two-1977, 1998

TURKEY

1. What is the capital city of Turkey?
2. What colours are on the flag of Turkey?
3. What is the official name of Turkey?
4. How many countries share a land border with Turkey?
5. What is the official language of Turkey?
6. What was Turkey known as before the current name?
7. What form of government does Turkey have?
8. Between 80 and 85 million, what is the population of Turkey?
9. Who is regarded as the founder of modern Turkey?
10. What was Turkey's status during World War Two?
11. What is the currency of Turkey?
12. Which country provides the most tourists to Turkey?
13. What is the largest city in Turkey?
14. Which side of the road do drivers in Turkey drive on?
15. What is the major religion in Turkey?
16. What is the most popular sport in Turkey?
17. How many times has Turkey won the Eurovision Song Contest?
18. Which country is the major export partner of Turkey?
19. Who is the Head of State and Head of the Government in Turkey?
20. What letters appear at the end of a web address from Turkey?
21. Which team from Turkey won the UEFA Cup and UEFA Super Cup in 2000?
22. Which is the largest ethnic minority in Turkey?

23. Which airline is the flag carrier of Turkey?
24. What side did Turkey fight with during World War One?
25. At which sport in the Summer Olympic Games has Turkey won the most medals?

TURKEY ANSWERS

1. Ankara
2. Red, white
3. Republic of Turkey
4. Seven-Bulgaria, Greece, Iran, Syria, Georgia, Iraq, Armenia
5. Turkish
6. Ottoman Empire
7. Presidential constitutional republic
8. 82 million (2018 estimate)
9. Mustafa Kemal Ataturk
10. Neutral
11. Turkish lira
12. Germany
13. Istanbul
14. Right hand side
15. Islam
16. Football
17. Once-2003
18. Germany
19. President
20. .tr
21. Galatasaray
22. Kurds
23. Turkish Airlines
24. Central Powers-Germany, Austria
25. Wrestling

UGANDA

1. What is the official name of Uganda?
2. What is the capital city of Uganda?
3. What colours are on the flag of Uganda?
4. How many countries share a land border with Uganda?
5. Which country did Uganda gain its independence from in 1962?
6. What are the two official languages of Uganda?
7. What form of government does Uganda have?
8. Between 40 and 45 million, what is the population of Uganda?
9. What is the currency of Uganda?
10. Which notorious general ruled Uganda as a dictator from 1971 to 1979?
11. Who is the Head of State in Uganda?
12. Which is the largest city in Uganda?
13. Uganda's international airport is in which city?
14. Which country is the major export partner of Uganda?
15. What is the dominant religious denomination in Uganda?
16. Who is the Head of Government in Uganda?
17. What is the main export commodity of Uganda?
18. Which sport has gained the most medals for Uganda at the Summer Olympic Games?
19. Which side of the road do drivers in Uganda drive on?
20. What is the national sport of Uganda?
21. What letters appear at the end of a web address from Uganda?
22. Which country is the major import partner of Uganda?

23. Which guerrilla leader of Uganda's northern region was the subject of a video that went viral in 2012?
24. Which large African lake is located in Uganda?
25. In which sport has Uganda won its two gold medals at the Summer Olympic Games?

UGANDA ANSWERS

1. Republic of Uganda
2. Kampala
3. Black, yellow, red
4. Five-Kenya, South Sudan, Democratic Republic of the Congo, Tanzania, Rwanda
5. United Kingdom
6. English, Swahili
7. Dominant party semi-presidential republic
8. 41 million (2016 estimate)
9. Ugandan shilling
10. Idi Amin
11. President
12. Kampala
13. Entebbe
14. Kenya
15. Roman Catholic
16. President
17. Coffee
18. Boxing
19. Left hand side
20. Football
21. .ug
22. China
23. Joseph Kony
24. Lake Victoria
25. Athletics

UKRAINE

1. What is the capital city of Ukraine?
2. What are the colours on the flag of Ukraine?
3. What is the official name of Ukraine?
4. Between 40 and 45 million, what is the population of Ukraine?
5. What form of government does Ukraine have?
6. What is the official language of Ukraine?
7. From which country did Ukraine gain its independence in 1991?
8. How many countries share a land border with Ukraine?
9. On which side did Ukraine fight with during World War One?
10. Who is the Head of State in Ukraine?
11. What is the currency of Ukraine?
12. What is the largest city in Ukraine?
13. Which country provides the most tourists to Ukraine?
14. Which side of the road do drivers in Ukraine drive on?
15. What is the main religion in Ukraine?
16. How many times has Ukraine won the Eurovision Song Contest?
17. What is the most popular sport in Ukraine?
18. What is the national food dish of Ukraine?
19. Which Ukrainian athlete was the world record holder in the pole vault for over ten years?
20. What letters appear at the end of a web address from Ukraine?
21. How many times have Ukraine films won the Academy Award for Best Foreign Language Film?

22. At which sport have Ukrainian athletes been most successful at the Summer Olympic Games?
23. Which chicken dish, named after Ukraine's capital city originated in Ukraine?
24. Who is the only Ukrainian footballer to win the Ballon d'Or football award?
25. Which group of people established a republic in the 17th and 18th centuries in Ukraine?

UKRAINE ANSWERS

1. Kiev
2. Blue, yellow
3. Ukraine
4. 42 million (2017 estimate)
5. Semi-presidential constitutional republic
6. Ukrainian
7. Soviet Union
8. Three-Belarus, Moldova, Russia
9. Both-Austro-Hungarian and Russian armies
10. President
11. Ukrainian hryvnia
12. Kiev
13. Moldova
14. Right hand side
15. Eastern Orthodox
16. Twice-204, 2016
17. Football
18. Borsch
19. Sergey Bubka
20. .ua
21. None
22. Gymnastics
23. Chicken Kiev
24. Andriy Shevchenko
25. Cossacks

UNITED ARAB EMIRATES (UAE)

1. How many emirates make up the UAE?
2. What is the capital city of the UAE?
3. What colours are on the flag of the UAE?
4. How many countries share a land border with the UAE?
5. What is the official name of the UAE?
6. What form of government does the UAE have?
7. What is the official language of the UAE?
8. In what year of the 1970s did the UAE become independent?
9. What is the dominant religion in the UAE?
10. Between five and ten million, what is the population of the UAE?
11. What is the main export of the UAE?
12. What is the largest city in the UAE?
13. What is the currency of the UAE?
14. Which UAE airport is the busiest in the world?
15. Which day in December is National Day in the UAE, marking Union Day of all the emirates?
16. What is the most popular sport in the UAE?
17. Where can people consume alcohol in the UAE?
18. Which side of the road to drivers in the UAE drive on?
19. What are the letters at the end of a web address from the UAE?
20. What is the second most popular sport in the UAE?
21. From which emirate does the President of the United Arab Emirates usually come from?
22. Which two countries are the UAE's largest export markets?

23. What is the dominant colour of each of the separate emirates of the UAE?
24. According to law, punishment of criminal offences in the UAE is between how many lashes?
25. Which UAE city is the headquarters of the ICC (International Cricket Council)?

UNITED ARAB EMIRATES (UAE) ANSWERS

1. Seven
2. Abu Dhabi
3. Green, red, white, black
4. Two-Saudi Arabia, Oman
5. United Arab Emirates
6. Constitutional monarchy (Absolute)
7. Arabic
8. 1971
9. Islam
10. Nine (.5) million (2018 estimate)
11. Oil
12. Dubai
13. UAE dirham
14. Dubai International Airport
15. December 2nd
16. Football
17. Bars, restaurants, private homes
18. Right hand side
19. .ae
20. Cricket
21. Abu Dhabi
22. United Kingdom, Germany
23. Red
24. 80-200 lashes
25. Dubai

UNITED KINGDOM

1. What is the official name for the United Kingdom?
2. What four countries make up the United Kingdom?
3. What is the capital of the United Kingdom?
4. What form of government does the United Kingdom have?
5. Which country shares a land border with the United Kingdom?
6. What is the official language of the United Kingdom?
7. Between 65 and 70 million, what is the population of the United Kingdom?
8. What is the currency of the United Kingdom?
9. Who was the Prime Minister of the United Kingdom for most of World War Two?
10. How many bodies of water surround the United Kingdom?
11. What are the colours on the flag of the United Kingdom?
12. Which side of the road do drivers in the United Kingdom drive on?
13. What is the most popular sport in the United Kingdom?
14. What letters are at the end of a web address from the United Kingdom?
15. What is the largest city in the United Kingdom?
16. How many Crown Dependencies and Overseas Territories does the United Kingdom have sovereignty over?
17. Who is the Head of State in the United Kingdom?
18. Which English playwright is regarded as the greatest dramatist of all time?
19. Which UK broadcaster is the oldest in the world?

20. How many times have countries from the United Kingdom hosted the Summer Olympic Games?
21. What is the name of the flag of the United Kingdom?
22. How many times has the United Kingdom won the Eurovision Song Contest?
23. Which country provides the most tourists to the United Kingdom?
24. In which year of the 1960s did England win the FIFA World Cup of football?
25. Which airline is the flag carrier in United Kingdom?

UNITED KINGDOM ANSWERS

1. United Kingdom of Great Britain and Northern Ireland
2. England, Scotland, Wales, Northern Ireland
3. London
4. Parliamentary democracy and Constitutional Monarchy
5. Republic of Ireland (with Northern Ireland)
6. English
7. 67 million (2019 estimate)
8. Pound Sterling
9. Winston Churchill
10. Five-Atlantic Ocean, North Sea, Irish Sea, English Channel, Celtic Sea
11. Red, white, blue
12. Left hand side
13. Football
14. .uk
15. London
16. Seventeen
17. Monarch
18. William Shakespeare
19. BBC (British Broadcasting Corporation)
20. Three times-1908, 1948, 2012
21. Union Flag (Union Jack)
22. Five
23. France
24. 1966
25. British Airways

UNITED STATES OF AMERICA

1. How many stars are on the United States flag?
2. Who was the first President of the United States?
3. In what year did the American colonies declare their independence from Great Britain?
4. Which American was the first man to walk on the surface of the moon?
5. What is the national language of the United States?
6. What is the currency of the United States?
7. What is the most popular spectator sport in the United States?
8. Which side of the road do American drivers drive on?
9. How many times has the United States hosted the Summer Olympic Games?
10. How many Americans have won the Nobel Prize for literature?
11. Which district of Los Angeles in the USA is a leading producer of motion pictures in the world?
12. Between 325 and 330 million, what is the population of the United States?
13. In what year did the United States enter the First World War?
14. Donald Trump is what number President of the United States?
15. What was the period of time called when it was illegal to sell, transport, produce and import alcohol in the United States?
16. What is the largest city in the United States?
17. What became the 50th state of the United States in 1959?

18. What is the capital of the United States?
19. Who became the first African-American President of the United States?
20. What is the national bird of the United States?
21. The American Civil War lasted between what years?
22. What is the name of the first National Park in the United States?
23. What is regarded as the national sport in the United States?
24. Which country provides the most tourists to the United States?
25. What is the most visited tourist attraction in the United States?

UNITED STATES OF AMERICA ANSWERS

1. 50 (One for each state)
2. George Washington
3. 1776 (July 4th)
4. Neil Armstrong
5. English
6. United States dollar
7. American football
8. Right hand side
9. Four times-St Louis, Los Angeles (twice), Atlanta
10. Twelve
11. Hollywood
12. 327 million (2018 estimate)
13. 1917
14. 45th President
15. Prohibition
16. New York City
17. Hawaii
18. Washington DC
19. Barack Obama
20. Bald eagle
21. 1861-1865
22. Yellowstone National Park
23. Baseball
24. Mexico
25. Times Square, New York City

URUGUAY

1. What is the official name of Uruguay?
2. What is the capital city of Uruguay?
3. How many countries share a land border with Uruguay?
4. What are the colours on the flag of Uruguay?
5. What is the official language of Uruguay?
6. Between one and five million, what is the population of Uruguay?
7. What form of government does Uruguay have?
8. What is the dominant religious denomination in Uruguay?
9. What is the currency of Uruguay?
10. From which country did Uruguay declare its independence in 1825?
11. Which country is the major import partner of Uruguay?
12. What percentage of Uruguay's electricity comes from renewables?
13. Who is the Head of State and Head of Government in Uruguay?
14. What is Uruguay's largest city?
15. What is the most popular sport in Uruguay?
16. Which country provides the most tourists to Uruguay?
17. Which side of the road do drivers in Uruguay drive on?
18. What letters appear at the end of a web address from Uruguay?
19. How many times has Uruguay won the FIFA World Cup of football?
20. Which country is Uruguay's major export partner?
21. What is Uruguay's national language?

22. In which sport has Uruguay won its two gold medals at the Summer Olympic Games?
23. What are the two main exports of Uruguay?
24. Who became the first Uruguayan to win an Academy Award in 2004, for Best Original Song from the film The Motorcycle Diaries?
25. Which Uruguayan footballer won the Golden Ball trophy as the best player at the 2010 FIFA World Cup of Football?

URUGUAY ANSWERS

1. Oriental Republic of Uruguay
2. Montevideo
3. Two-Brazil, Argentina
4. Blue, white
5. Spanish
6. 3 (.4) million (2016 estimate)
7. Presidential constitutional republic
8. Roman Catholicism
9. Uruguayan peso
10. Brazil
11. China
12. 95%
13. President
14. Montevideo
15. Football
16. Argentina
17. Right hand side
18. .uy
19. Twice-1930, 1950
20. China
21. Spanish
22. Football
23. Beef, soya beans
24. Jorge Drexler
25. Diego Forlan

VATICAN CITY

1. What is the official name for the Vatican City?
2. What is the capital city of the Vatican City?
3. What colours are on the flag of the Vatican City?
4. In what year of the 1920s did the Vatican City become independent?
5. Within which city is the Vatican City an enclave?
6. What is the official language of the Vatican City?
7. What form of government does the Vatican City have?
8. Between 1000 and 5000, what is the population of the Vatican City?
9. What was the policy of the Vatican City during World War II?
10. Where does the Vatican City rate in terms of area and population of countries in the world?
11. Who is the sovereign of the Vatican City?
12. What is the currency of the Vatican City?
13. What are the major crimes in the Vatican City?
14. What is the formal name of the central government of the Catholic Church?
15. What is the largest city in the Vatican City?
16. Which side of the road do drivers in the Vatican City drive on?
17. What industry is the major revenue source for Vatican City?
18. What is the dominant religion of the Vatican City?
19. Which language is often used in documents in the Vatican City?

20. Which church in the Vatican City is home to some of the most famous art work?
21. In kilometres, how long and wide is the Vatican City?
22. What letters appear at the end of a web address from the Vatican City?
23. What is the official residence of the Pope in the Vatican City?
24. How many teams are in the Vatican City Championship in football?
25. What was the name of the treaty that established the city-state of the Vatican City?

VATICAN CITY ANSWERS

1. Vatican City State
2. Vatican City
3. Yellow, white
4. 1929
5. Rome
6. Italian
7. Absolute monarchy under an ecclesiastical and elective theocracy
8. 1000 (2017 estimate)
9. Neutral
10. Smallest in area and population
11. The Pope
12. Euro
13. Pickpocketing, bag snatching
14. Holy See
15. Vatican City
16. Right hand side
17. Sale of postage stamps and tourist mementos
18. Roman Catholic
19. Latin
20. St Peter's Basilica
21. 1.05km long x 0.85km wide
22. .va
23. Sistine Chapel
24. Eight
25. Lateran Treaty

VENEZUELA

1. What is the capital city of Venezuela?
2. What is the official name of Venezuela?
3. In which continent is Venezuela?
4. How many countries share a land border with Venezuela?
5. What colours are on the flag of Venezuela?
6. What is the official language of Venezuela?
7. What is the dominant religious denomination of Venezuela?
8. What form of government does Venezuela have?
9. From which country did Venezuela gain its independence in 1811?
10. Which is the world's highest waterfall, located in Venezuela?
11. Who is the Head of State in Venezuela?
12. What is Venezuela's major export commodity?
13. What is the currency of Venezuela?
14. Between 30 and 35 million, what is the population of Venezuela?
15. Which country is the major export partner of Venezuela?
16. What is the most popular sport in Venezuela?
17. Which side of the road do drivers in Venezuela drive on?
18. Who is the Head of Government in Venezuela?
19. How many stars are on the flag of Venezuela?
20. Which country is the major import partner of Venezuela?
21. Which former military officer was President of Venezuela from 1999 until his death in 2013?
22. Which rainforest is partially located in Venezuela?

23. In which sport has Venezuela gained the bulk of its medals at the Summer Olympic Games?
24. Which letters appear at the end of a web address from Venezuela?
25. What is the largest city in Venezuela?

VENEZUELA ANSWERS

1. Caracas
2. Bolivarian Republic of Venezuela
3. South America
4. Three-Colombia, Brazil, Guyana
5. Yellow, blue red
6. Spanish
7. Roman Catholic
8. Federal presidential constitutional republic
9. Spain
10. Angel Falls
11. President
12. Oil, petroleum products
13. Bolivar Soberano
14. 31 million (2016 estimate)
15. United States of America
16. Baseball
17. Right hand side
18. President
19. Eight white stars
20. United States of America
21. Hugo Chavez
22. Amazon Rainforest
23. Boxing
24. .ve
25. Caracas

VIETNAM

1. What are the colours of the Vietnamese flag?
2. In what year was Vietnam reunified?
3. What is the official name of Vietnam?
4. What is the capital of Vietnam?
5. What is the official language of Vietnam?
6. Vietnam was a colony of which European country until 1945?
7. Between 90 and 95 million, what is the population of Vietnam?
8. Which side of the road to the Vietnamese drivers drive on?
9. What is the largest city in Vietnam?
10. Which major country sent troops to fight in the Vietnam War in 1965?
11. How many stars are on the flag of Vietnam?
12. What is the most popular sport in Vietnam?
13. In which sport did Vietnam win its first Gold Medal at the Summer Olympic Games?
14. What was the capital city of the former South Vietnam?
15. What is the main religion in Vietnam?
16. How many countries share a land border with Vietnam?
17. What letters are at the end of a web address from Vietnam?
18. Who was the leader of the North Vietnamese for the majority of the Vietnam War?
19. In what year did Vietnam first compete at the Summer Olympic Games?
20. What is considered the most important celebration in Vietnamese culture?

21. What is the main airline in Vietnam?

22. What are the three most popular forms of road transport that are used in Vietnam?

23. Which country is the biggest importer of Vietnamese goods?

24. Apart from Vietnam, which is the only other communist state in South East Asia?

25. Which herbicide is the main environmental concern in Vietnam?

VIETNAM ANSWERS

1. Red and yellow
2. 1976
3. Socialist Republic of Vietnam
4. Hanoi
5. Vietnamese
6. France
7. 94 million (2016 estimate)
8. Right hand side
9. Ho Chi Minh City
10. United States of America
11. One
12. Football
13. Shooting
14. Saigon
15. Vietnamese folk religion (irreligious)
16. Four-China, Thailand, Laos, Cambodia
17. .vn
18. Ho Chi Minh
19. 1988
20. Tet (Vietnamese New Year)
21. Vietnam Airlines
22. Bicycles, motorcycles, motor scooters
23. United States of America
24. Laos
25. Agent Orange

WALES

1. What is the official name of Wales?
2. What is the capital city of Wales?
3. What colours are on the flag of Wales?
4. Between one and five million, what is the population of Wales?
5. How many countries share a land border with Wales?
6. What are the official languages of Wales?
7. What sovereign country is Wales part of?
8. Which Welsh politician was the last Liberal Prime Minister of the United Kingdom?
9. What form of government does Wales have?
10. What currency does Wales have?
11. What sport is seen as a symbol of Welsh identity?
12. Who is the Head of State in Wales?
13. Which is the largest island off the coast of Wales?
14. What is the largest city in Wales?
15. Who is the leader of the Welsh government?
16. Which side of the road do drivers in Wales drive on?
17. What symbol is on the flag of Wales?
18. At which sporting games does Wales compete as a separate nation?
19. What industry transformed Wales from an agricultural society to an industrial one?
20. What is the dominant religious denomination in Wales?
21. Who is the Patron Saint of Wales?
22. Who have been the most successful male and female singers to come from Wales?

23. How many Welsh teams play football in the English Football League?
24. Which long-running British science fiction series has been filmed in Wales?
25. Which Welsh cyclist won the 2018 Tour de France?

WALES ANSWERS

1. Wales
2. Cardiff
3. Red, white, green
4. 3 million (2017 estimate)
5. One-England
6. Welsh, English
7. Great Britain/United Kingdom
8. David Lloyd-George
9. Devolved parliamentary legislature
10. Pound sterling
11. Rugby union
12. Monarch-Queen Elizabeth II
13. Anglesey
14. Cardiff
15. First Minister
16. Left hand side
17. A dragon
18. Commonwealth Games
19. Mining
20. Church in Wales
21. Saint David
22. Tom Jones, Shirley Bassey
23. Six-Cardiff City, Swansea City, Newport County, Wrexham, Colwyn Bay, Merthyr Town
24. Doctor Who
25. Geraint Thomas

ZIMBABWE

1. How many official languages does Zimbabwe have?
2. What are the colours on the flag of Zimbabwe?
3. What is the capital of Zimbabwe?
4. What is the official name of Zimbabwe?
5. For how many years was Robert Mugabe the President of Zimbabwe?
6. Between 15 and 20 million, what is the population of Zimbabwe?
7. What was the previous name for Zimbabwe?
8. From which country did Zimbabwe gain its independence in 1980?
9. How many countries share a land border with Zimbabwe?
10. Which currency was suspended in Zimbabwe due to hyperinflation?
11. Which country provides the most tourists to Zimbabwe?
12. What is the largest city in Zimbabwe?
13. What is the national emblem of Zimbabwe?
14. What is the most popular sport in Zimbabwe?
15. Which Zimbabwean golfer was ranked number one in the world for 43 weeks in the 1990s?
16. On which side of the road do the drivers in Zimbabwe drive?
17. What are the letters that appear at the end of a web address from Zimbabwe?
18. What is the official currency used by the government of Zimbabwe?
19. Which waterfall is a major tourist attraction in Zimbabwe?

20. What is the main language spoken in the education and judiciary systems?
21. Of the 80% of Christians in Zimbabwe, what is the major religious denomination?
22. Kirsty Coventry has been Zimbabwe's most successful Olympian. At what sport was she an Olympic champion?
23. What colour is the star on the flag of Zimbabwe?
24. How many provinces are there in Zimbabwe?
25. Zimbabwe has large deposits of which valuable metal?

ZIMBABWE ANSWERS

1. Sixteen
2. Red, yellow, black, green, white
3. Harare
4. Republic of Zimbabwe
5. 30 years-1987-2017
6. 16 million (2016 estimate)
7. Rhodesia (Southern Rhodesia)
8. United Kingdom
9. Four-South Africa, Botswana, Zambia, Mozambique
10. Zimbabwean dollar
11. South Africa
12. Harare
13. Zimbabwe bird
14. Football-soccer
15. Nick Price
16. Left hand side
17. .zw
18. US Dollar
19. Victoria Falls
20. English
21. Protestant
22. Swimming
23. Red
24. Ten (Eight provinces + two cities with provincial status)
25. Platinum

Printed in the USA
CPSIA information can be obtained
at www.ICGtesting.com
LVHW090719131123
763762LV00003B/20